DANDY★DON MEREDITH

THE FIRST DALLAS COWBOY

DANDY DON MEREDITH

AUTOGRAPH

YANKEE
COWBOY
PUBLISHING

DANDY ★ DON MEREDITH

THE FIRST DALLAS COWBOY
DAVE LIEBER

ALSO BY DAVE LIEBER

AMON! The Ultimate Texan
(book and play)

The Dog of My Nightmares:
Stories by Texas Columnist Dave Lieber

Dave Lieber's Watchdog Nation:
Bite Back When Businesses and
Scammers Do You Wrong

Searching for Perot:
My Journey to Discover
Texas' Top Family
(book and play)

"I've always known who I was. I'm Billy Jack's little brother, Jeff and Hazel's baby boy, and I'm from Mount Vernon, Texas."

—Don Meredith

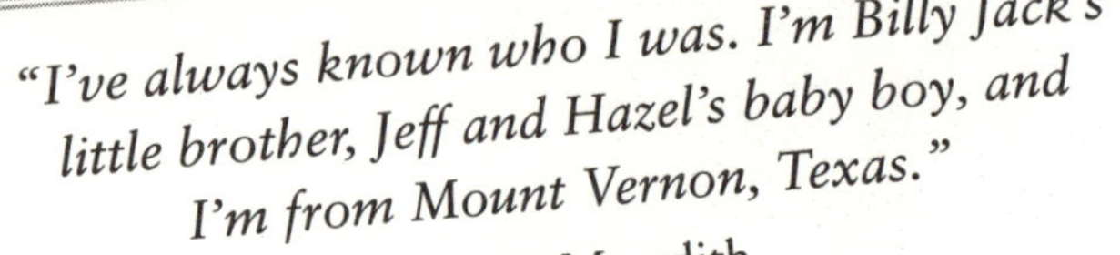

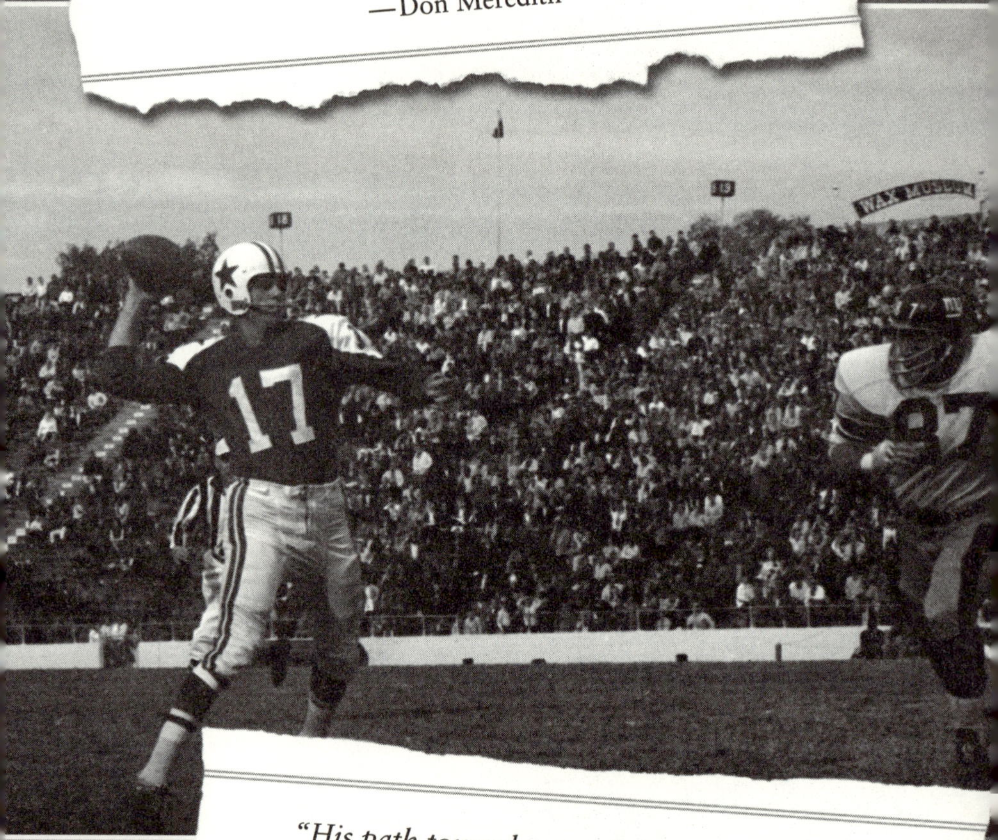

"His path toward unreachable glory resembled the classical mythical journey: Assigned impossible tasks, subjected to merciless trials, he soldiered on, a hero who sacrificed himself so his successors might win."

—writer Curt Sampson in a 2010 *D Magazine* profile

Contents

INTRODUCTION

WHEN DAVE LIEBER asked me to edit *Dandy Don Meredith — The First Dallas Cowboy*, I felt as if my life had almost come full circle.

First, let's get one thing straight. Unlike others, I never booed Don Meredith. He was my first and favorite football hero.

Growing up in Grand Prairie, Texas, in the early 1960s, on Sunday afternoons we'd usually pile into my grandparents' white Ford Galaxie 500 for a drive after church and lunch. The radio would be on, and if it was a fall afternoon, we'd tune to the Dallas Cowboys broadcast. As we listened, my dad and granddad explained various intricacies of football to a 5-year-old, like why teams had four downs to make 10 yards but usually punted on fourth down.

Pretty soon those Sunday afternoon drives became Sunday afternoon gatherings in front of the TV as we joined the growing number of Cowboys fans. Sometimes we'd find the Cotton Bowl end zone — $5 general admission for my dad, $1 for me — to watch our bunch of lovable losers.

Most lovable of them all was Don Meredith, Jeff and Hazel's baby boy from Mount Vernon in East Texas. To me, he was a winner. Even to a first-grader, he was charismatic, his competitiveness and leadership evident. But he also was fun. Who wouldn't love a quarterback who sang in the huddle?

I never missed his weekly television show, and one time I wrote in with a question. I don't remember the question, but I remember the result: a thank you postcard from Don Meredith! It's still one of my prized possessions.

I always wanted Dandy Don to "go for the bomb" to Bob Hayes, and often he'd oblige, even if it was incomplete.

As the Cowboys got better, my fandom got stronger. Didn't everyone's? I lived and died with them. I also was becoming more aware of Meredith's challenges—the booing and the criticism from the press and his coach. We took two or three newspapers a day, and I devoured the stories about Don and the Cowboys from sports journalism legends like Blackie Sherrod and Frank Luksa. Little did I know that one day I would work in the same newsrooms with them.

Third-grade me vividly remembers the Ice Bowl in 1967—the questions early in the day about whether the game would even be played—and the disbelief that it actually was. When it was over, I went in the bathroom and cried.

Meredith was out of football two years, but in 1970 he was back—on "Monday Night Football" as the foil for Howard Cosell. My dad and I were among those in the Cotton Bowl stands for his return to Dallas as an analyst in a 38-0 Cardinals blowout. I was one of those shouting, "We want Meredith!" at him in the press box.

My Meredith fandom stretched through the '70s and '80s as I followed his forays into TV ("Police Story") and the movies. My favorite flick? *Banjo Hackett, Roaming Free*, starring Meredith as a folksy 1880s horse trader. In those days, whether in sports, television or as a pitchman, he was ubiquitous.

And then he disappeared. As an editor at *The Dallas Morning News*, I followed Brad Townsend's efforts to land an interview and rejoiced at the rare access he received in 2009.

I always wondered why Meredith never wrote a book or why someone hadn't written a book about him. What a character he was. He also set the standard for Cowboys quarterbacks—win on the field, then hit the broadcast booth. Staubach, White, Aikman and Romo followed, with varying degrees of success and longevity.

In the end, there's only one Don Meredith. And Dave Lieber's fascinating look at his life finally tells the whole story of the first Cowboy. I hope you have as much fun reading this book as I did editing it.

—Mede Nix

CHAPTER 1

UNDER THE LIGHTS

PEOPLE MAY think the debut of ABC's "Monday Night Football" marked the first time football was played under the lights at night. They're off 78 years. The original night game was at the 1892 Great Mansfield Fair in Tioga County, Pennsylvania. Attendees were promised that they would see electric lights brighten the night sky. Thomas Edison, who had invented the modern light bulb 13 years earlier and created General Electric, sent his Thomson-Huston machine with its 30-bulb capacity.

The teams were Mansfield State Normal and Wyoming Seminary. At sunset a pole carrying lights was moved to the middle of the darkening field. Soon difficult to see the players, the referee called the game. Final score: 0-0.

Flash forward to September 1970. A different kind of historic nighttime football is about to launch. A bevy of naysayers—the press, network executives, National Football League team owners—believe ABC's vanity project, "Monday Night Football," will fail.

The show, created by television legend Roone Arledge, is designed to break all the sports broadcasting rules, beginning with: Events must have two announcers. Arledge wanted three.

The first play-by-play announcer on MNF would be Keith Jackson, ol' reliable no matter the sport. (Frank Gifford would replace him in season two.) The second man in the booth would be Howard Cosell, credited as the inventor of hard-hitting TV sports journalism and, for various reasons (his support of Muhammad Ali chief among them), perhaps the most hated man on TV. Who to compare him to? No one comes close. Picture Steven A. Smith as a white, Jewish Brooklyn lawyer with an annoying staccato voice and a toupee.

The third man in the booth? Don Meredith, former quarterback for the Dallas Cowboys. Born in Mount Vernon, Texas, Meredith was no stranger to those Americans who followed NFL football. What nobody saw besides Arledge was that the Northern lawyer and the Southern quarterback would become the most liked American comedy team since Dean Martin and Jerry Lewis. Nobody said a football game had to be serious, Arledge complained. "I'm tired of football being treated like a religion. The games aren't played in Westminster Abbey."

"Monday Night Football," given the comedic conflicts between Cosell and Meredith, rocketed to the top of the ratings. The show was a monster hit, changed the way sports are covered on TV and gave its first profit in a decade.

When the vast MNF production team rolled into an NFL city before a game, it was as big as the game itself. The announcers often received the keys to the city. Banquets were held in their honor. What teams were playing? Didn't matter. Cosell and Meredith were in town! Meredith dubbed it Mother Love's Traveling Freak Show.

But before the Sept. 21, 1970, on-air debut, there was a practice game involving the Lions and the Chiefs. This rehearsal was never broadcast. Good thing. Mother Love was not pleased.

Arledge told what happened in his autobiography, *Roone: A Memoir.*

"Don had problems. He was talking in clichés. ('Hello football fans everywhere.') Using 10 sentences to say what could be said in three, analyzing the obvious, and because he hadn't done his homework, having a tough time keeping track of who was whom and on which team."

Hearing this criticism, Meredith stood, threw down his earpiece and said, "Screw this." He acted as if he'd leave. Everyone convinced him to stay.

The next day, after a second harsh critique, it happened again.

"Look, fellas," he said, "this really isn't my bag, and I don't even know that much about football. I only know the X's and O's Mr. [Tom] Landry taught me in Texas. So I'll just leave."

Arledge and MNF director Chet Forte made it clear to Meredith that this was a natural process and that their notes were only suggestions for improvement.

Meredith left and Cosell ran after him. He persuaded Meredith to have a drink before he left for the airport. Then in a reminder of his signature phrase — "tell it like it is" — Cosell tried to do just that.

"Don," Cosell said, according to his autobiography, *Cosell*, "in my opinion you'll be making the biggest mistake of your life if you even think about leaving us. You're going to come out of this a hero. Middle America will love you. Southern America will love you. And there are at least 40 sportswriters in this country who can't wait to get at me. You'll benefit thereby. Don't worry about me, though, because in the long run it will work for the old coach, too. You'll wear the white hat. I'll wear the black hat, and you'll have no problems from the very beginning."

All of which turned out to be 100% accurate.

"Dandy lifted his glass," Cosell wrote, and said, "By golly. I'm with you, Coach. All the way."

The dream team with (from left) Howard Cosell, Don Meredith and Frank Gifford.

On debut night, at precisely 9 Eastern time, the flashy opening video showed the countdown in the game truck outside. It focused on the inner workings of the production team, sending a message that this game would be different.

Jackson opened: "From Municipal Stadium in Cleveland, Ohio, two powers in professional football meet for the first time ever as members of the new American Conference of the National Football League." He introduced the sponsors, Ford, Marlboro and Goodyear.

Then Cosell did a welcome: "It's a hot, sultry, almost windless night where the Browns will play host to the New York Jets. Good evening, everyone. I'm Howard Cosell, and welcome to ABC's Monday night prime-time National Football League series."

What happened next surprised Meredith. He heard "roll the tape" in his earpiece, then saw a video montage of his time as the Cowboys' quarterback. It showed his sacks, interceptions, fumbles and botched handoffs. ABC did it to "set up Meredith's comic persona," according to co-authors Marc Gunther and Bill Carter in their book *Monday Night Mayhem: The Inside Story Behind ABC's Monday Night Football.*

"The gag worked," they wrote. "It sparked sympathy immediately for the just-folks new announcer, even if it presented a grossly distorted picture of Meredith's mostly stellar career on the field.

"Meredith didn't know he was going to be roasted in the film clip, but his aw-shucks reaction furnished the first impression: Cosell came on sour; Meredith came on sweet. Black hat/white hat. An act was born."

With that, the revolution in TV sports coverage began. Less rah-rah. More inside news, even if embarrassing. No evading controversial subjects. Always trying, on Cosell's part, to ask the most difficult questions.

Now was the time to shine for the ex-player who introduced himself to America on Monday nights this way: "I'm Billy Jack's little brother, Jeff and Hazel's baby boy, and I'm from Mount Vernon, Texas."

Meredith would become one of the most famous and beloved men in America. But that would take a few more weeks.

CHAPTER 2

SWINGING TIRE

GO BACK to the beginning. This epic started in the most unassuming of settings—a tire, suspended like a pendulum from the sturdy branches of a pecan tree.

In this saga, a little boy crippled with polio in infancy recovered and went on to enjoy athletic glory, broadcasting success and, finally, acting stardom. He helped change TV coverage of sports.

It grew from the boy's parents hanging a tire and an old quilt behind it to serve as a backstop. Over and over, the boy threw a football at that tire target. That's how Dandy Don Meredith launched his career as a quarterback.

The story of Joseph Don Meredith, born April 10, 1938, is legendary. He went from polio victim to most popular boy in high school (where he was named All-State) to college All-American to starting quarterback for "America's Team." It's a story of a man with great gifts—extraordinary sense of humor, good looks, sexy East Texas twang and a natural leadership style that worked no matter where his feet were planted.

Back to that swinging tire.

"It wasn't enough that I had to throw the football through the tire and hope the quilt would stop it," he once explained. "But my mother would give it a swing. I'd have to lead the tire. There was a rut worn in the grass from me dropping back to throw."

At Mount Vernon Elementary School in his hometown, school officials were thinking ahead. Don's older brother, Billy Jack, played quarterback and eventually started for the TCU Horned Frogs. Somebody figured that Don could one day play QB, too.

When Meredith was in the third grade, the district's bus driver, Narvel Lawrence, was asked to play catch with him every day during last period, which Meredith was allowed to skip. The goal was to teach him how to throw and strengthen

Hazel and Jeff Meredith are among the most famous parents in the nation. Their son says their name, in some context, on almost every "Monday Night Football" telecast.

his arm. Off they'd go to chuck the ball back and forth. After much practice he could toss a football across the field with precision.

In each step toward fame Meredith faced stiff obstacles—physical, mental and emotional.

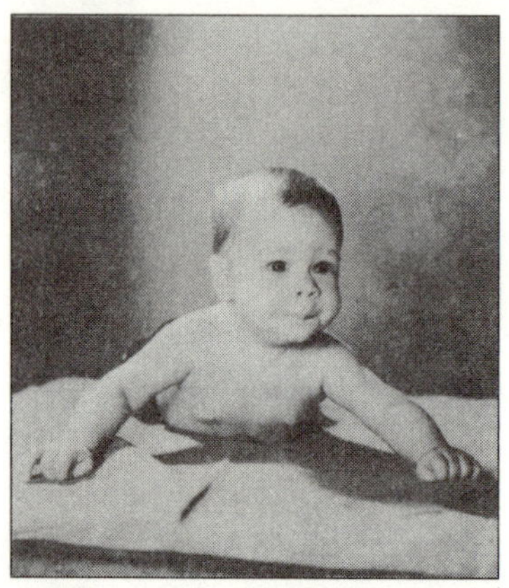

It never came up, but Baby Don had polio as an infant and spent at least seven months in his crib.

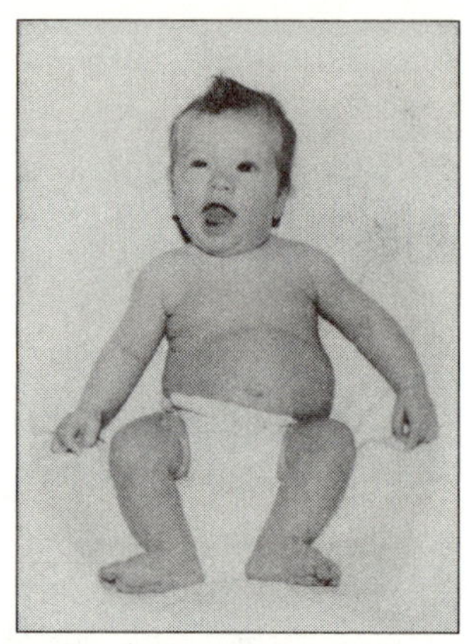

Little Don gets stronger as he grows.

Don as a toddler.

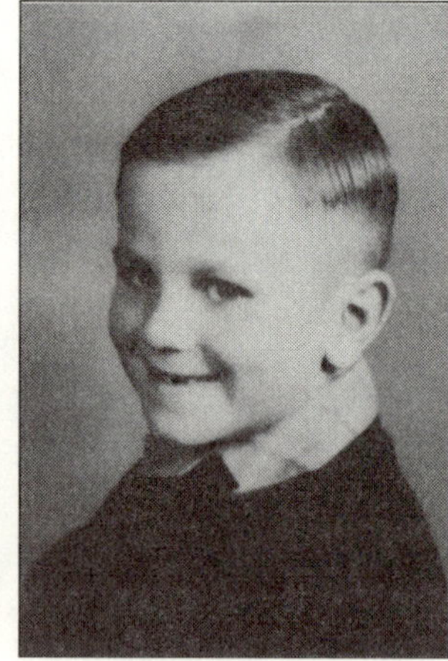

Don, 8 years old, in the 4th grade.

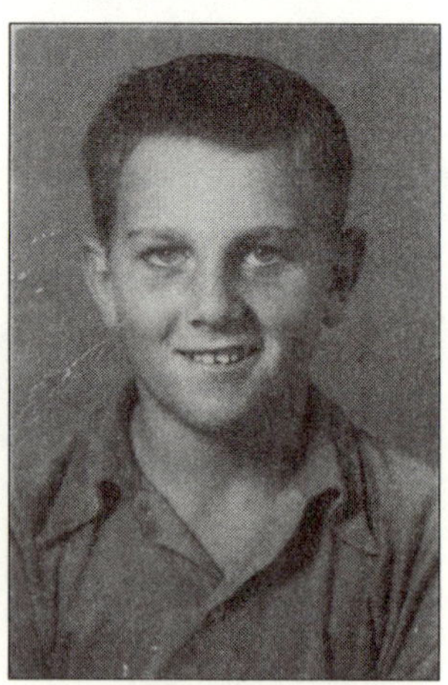

Don is starting to look like, well, Don.

Childhood photos of Don from SMU Archives, DeGolyer Library, Southern Methodist University

Writer Curt Sampson penned a 2010 *D Magazine* profile, with almost the same title as this book, that well described Meredith's journey: "His path toward unreachable glory resembled the classical mythical journey: Assigned impossible tasks, subjected to merciless trials, he soldiered on, a hero who sacrificed himself so his successors might win."

CHAPTER 3

GROWING UP IN MOUNT VERNON

MEREDITH ENJOYED a near perfect life in Mount Vernon (current population around 2,500), a town 100 miles northeast of Dallas.

His biggest setback was polio, which kept him in the crib, according to Curt Sampson's reporting in that 2010 *D Magazine* story. Following recovery, his calves would always be thinner, which made him self-conscious—and more prone to injury.

For his son's first job, Jeff Meredith put his boy, then around 6, on the front counter of his store, Meredith Dry Goods, and told him what to do.

"Son, when you see people come in that door, you greet 'em by name. Even a dog likes to hear his name."

Running a store and raising cattle didn't make the family rich. "I didn't realize we were poor until I was 18 because everything had been so smooth," the younger Meredith said. "We always ate well, and my jeans and T-shirts were always clean, but we never really had any money."

Meredith was grateful for what he had. In the town's history book, *Memories of Don Meredith and Hometown Mount Vernon*, a neighbor recalled overhearing how he once complimented his mother, Hazel: "You have taught it, every bit, to me Mother. You have helped me so much. I'm glad to do what I can for you."

He was class president, lead actor in the school's one-act play, active in 4-H (where he and his team won a state shrubbery identification contest), and a member of Future Farmers of America. And he sang in the Methodist church choir.

Two stories in the town history book foreshadow traits he would later show as a pro football player—rebelliousness against authority and loyalty to his teammates.

In high school, someone brought a cherry bomb to study hall and threw it against the floor to make it explode. But it didn't. Meredith asked if he could try. After all, he liked to throw things with power.

"Let me see that thing," he said.

BOOM!

Principal Rufus Bolger and other teachers tried to hunt down the culprit, asking every student, "Did you do it? Do you know who did?" No one snitched.

The basketball coach announced that if a member of his team did it, he'd be off the squad.

Asked the same questions, Meredith didn't hesitate: "Yes sir, I did it." He was not forced to quit the basketball team, his classmates were loyal to him, and he showed complete honesty.

Still, he got paddled. "It's the American way," the principal would say later.

Meredith was allowed to play basketball. His honesty and loyalty were two traits that would continue to serve him well.

In the second story, Gladys Lawrence, his third-grade teacher, recalled that Meredith "had the best manners and was really the nicest child I ever taught." But there was this one time. He had turned around, and she asked him to face the front of the room. When he didn't, she said, "I want to see you at recess."

"I made him write 'I will obey my teacher' several times. I forget how many. He pouted for a couple of days, and then everything was all right again."

He was a good student but he really excelled at sports. "I have been a star since I was six," he told *Parade* magazine in a 1983 interview. "I was the youngest kid on the school team. Whenever we chose up sides to play I was the one who always chose. Then everybody wanted to be on my side."

Edson Reynolds tells this story in the town history book: "He was coming down the sidewalk toward the store and our car. I said, 'Here comes Don Meredith.'" Reynolds' 5-year-old daughter, Lynn, "fluffed the back of her hair with her hand and replied, 'Oh, my goodness, and my hair is a mess!'"

The senior class president had an aura. No one was surprised when he was elected Mr. Mount Vernon High. "Girls saw him as a real charmer," the town history book states. "Boys followed his leadership faithfully both on and off the athletic fields."

Classmate John Stinson recalls that "one time there was a girl, sorta poor. Guess you could call her underprivileged. That was before the school had a cafeteria, and everyone carried a lunch. She always brought a biscuit and onion for lunch. You know how kids are. They were making fun of her, and Don got up and went over there and sat down and ate part of her lunch with her. The kids didn't make fun of her anymore."

Stinson said people followed Meredith's lead. "If he came out with a new pair of shoes, it kind of set a fad."

This was the mid-1950s—crewcuts, blue jeans rolled up, white socks and penny loafers—and for those lucky enough, a leather sports letter jacket. Picture Meredith as an East Texas James Dean, minus the alienation.

Of course, he quarterbacked the football team, and he also played middle linebacker and was a left-footed punter and kicker. In his junior year against arch-rival Winnsboro, he threw three touchdown passes, ran for two touchdowns, kicked two extra points and intercepted a pass. He was named All-State.

Big things were expected of him his senior year. But in the fifth game, Meredith broke his collarbone and was out for the season. The team didn't win another game.

Basketball was his true love. He was all razzle-dazzle with a graceful hook shot. Pregame in the high school gym, instead of normal layup drills, Meredith stood on the free-throw line, whistled loudly and scooted the ball to his teammates with showmanship worthy of the Harlem Globetrotters. "The Don Meredith drill," coach Wayne Pierce called it.

Sampson wrote, "With Meredith grinning, standing by himself at the free-throw line, someone threw him the ball, and he took it between his legs and down his arms and around his waist in hypnotic circles and figure eights, then threw improbable no-look passes" to his teammates.

Pierce was a tough coach. Meredith's longtime friend Ken Greer told me how Pierce conditioned his players using a red broom. On defense, the team played a full-court press the entire game, so everybody was always running.

"He would buy a broom each year and cut it off so he would have half of it. "He would condition them by chasing them down the court," Greer told me. Whoever was last felt the power of the broom.

Whap! Whap!

Miss free throws?

Whap! Whap!

"It was a different time," Greer said.

In his junior year, the Tigers traveled to Dallas for the 1954 Dr Pepper Cotton Bowl Invitational Tournament, and

Under Don's leadership, the Mount Vernon Tigers win the Dr Pepper basketball tournament in Dallas. Don is even better at basketball than football. He earns All-State honors. Notice he's the tallest on the team and his socks are pulled up higher than the others because he is self-conscious.

Meredith made statewide news. *The Dallas Morning News* reported that he scored so many points, he was a "basket cramming junior." Playing center against W.H. Adamson High, he scored an all-time tournament record 52 points in one game, and the Tigers won 90-36. As the game MVP Meredith took home a metal Dr Pepper ice chest.

One writer noted that he wore knee pads around his shins, "obscuring his birdy legs."

In the next game, his Tigers played tournament favorite and defending champion Crozier Tech. The little 2A school knocked off the much larger 4A school to win the

Check out the height advantage. At the tournament Don set a record for most points in a game and most in the entire tournament. He went to Southern Methodist University on a basketball scholarship, not for football.

championship. Meredith's 164 points in five games set another tournament record that lasted decades. He was named to the All-State basketball team.

On graduation day, he was one of four speakers. In boxes of papers his third wife, Susan, donated to the DeGolyer Library at Southern Methodist University in 2019, I found a commencement speech that I presume is the one Meredith made as class salutatorian.

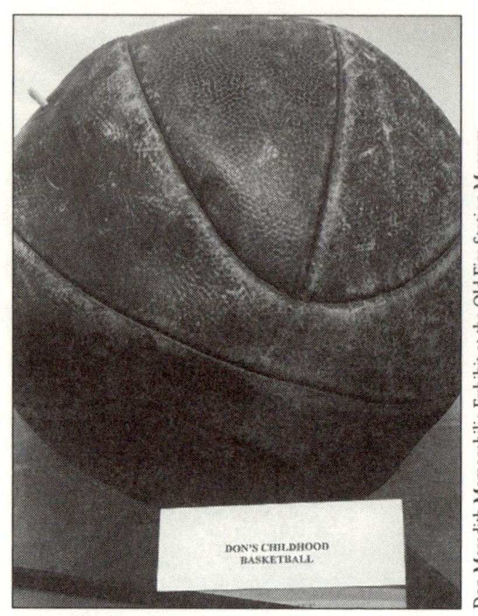

During high school team warm-ups,
Don dazzles the audience with ball tricks
performed with his teammates.
This is his childhood ball.

Highlights: "We who stand tonight at the meeting between a happy past and an unknown future have reached not the end, but the commencement of our lives. What those lives are to be depends in a large measure upon the foundations we have laid thus far in life. Classmates, what a big thought it is that from this time on we have the shaping of our destinies in our own hands.

"The one thing that we should strive for in life is true happiness. What we do for others is what makes happiness and success. If you know a person who is in need of help and you render your services unto him, you will realize what true happiness is."

He could have no idea how true his prophecy would be.

CHAPTER 4

SOUTHERN MEREDITH UNIVERSITY

MANY COLLEGES sought the two-time All-State basketball and football star, including Texas A&M (coached by Bear Bryant), Oklahoma, Arkansas, Louisiana, West Point, Colorado, Notre Dame, UCLA, Texas and SMU in Dallas.

Schools promised Meredith gifts galore if he accepted admission. A lawyer offered to fully fund law school (a Meredith dream), pay him $1,000 a month in the off-season (that's equivalent to $11,000 today) and buy him a car. One university offered to make his high school coach an assistant dorm director.

He picked SMU because it was "closer to home and easy to spell." Similar to his popularity in high school, he carried a certain aura. He was voted freshman class president.

He received a full-ride scholarship, but for basketball, which he never got to play.

He broke his ankle playing freshman football. "I still wanted to," he said in a 1978 *Playboy* magazine interview. "I went out for the team in my sophomore year. My illusion of playing big-time basketball was thrown back into my face about as rapidly as my hook shot was."

He decided to focus on football, except he was way down on the depth chart. Some published accounts had him third string; others put him as low as seventh, with six quarterbacks ahead of him.

To at least get him in the game, the coach put him at middle linebacker. One by one, the QBs fell off. One signed a baseball contract. Another got hurt. Sooner than expected in his sophomore year, Meredith was starting QB.

In the seventh game of the 1957 season, when he was only a sophomore, he suddenly was quarterback in the big-time Southwest Conference. His Mustangs were playing the Texas Longhorns at Memorial Stadium in Austin. It was coach Darrell Royal's first season. Some 39 years later, the stadium would be renamed after him. But this was not a good day for Royal and his Longhorns.

SMU's new quarterback was on fire. He threw two touchdown passes, ran for a third and carried

A promotional photo for SMU's star quarterback.

the ball 10 times for 72 yards. SMU upset an overconfident UT 19-12.

Until his graduation, Meredith was the school's No. 1 QB. In his first year he led the nation with a stunning 69% pass completion rate. One writer said the offense "depended on his uncanny knack of avoiding tacklers."

"I sort of ran all over the place and then usually threw the ball," he recalled. "I hated regimentation."

He solidified his standing that first season with two more unexpected victories against highly regarded Baylor and Arkansas.

Against Arkansas he was 19 of 25 passing with two TDs. He ran for two more touchdowns and kicked the final extra point in the 27-22 win. He also returned a kickoff 34 yards.

Courtesy of *The Fort Worth Star-Telegram* Collection, Special Collections, The University of Texas at Arlington Libraries

SMU players rush to congratulate Meredith, No. 17, after he throws a touchdown pass in the fourth quarter during an October 1958 game against Georgia Tech.

This upset knocked the Razorbacks out of the national rankings.

What couldn't Don Meredith do?

The student newspaper quoted an unnamed team coach who said, "I have never seen any sophomore who showed so much poise. Never. He has the greatest potential of any back I've ever watched."

Student newspaper editor Jay Brown asked in a column, "Is Meredith a valid grid-iron sensation or a flash in the pan?… Seldom is it that a sophomore establishes himself with such fiery rapidity and in such a spectacular manner."

The newspaper called him a "a tall, strong tailback, with a sense of poise which matches men twice his age."

SMU fans are proud of their star player leading the nation in throwing accuracy.

"Football was fun at SMU," he would say later. "We'd make up plays in the huddle, and that was fine with our coach.... I was definitely a hot dog, and I loved to hot dog around.... One of my favorite plays was real simple. I'd say, 'OK, hike the ball, and let's see who can get open.'"

As an All American in 1958 and 1959, he broke the NCAA record for career passing accuracy with 61%. All that training with the tire and the school bus driver surely paid off.

His team wasn't as sharp, though. His last season, his senior year, the Mustangs were 5-4-1; the year before they were 6-4.

He got used to crowds. For the 1959 season SMU drew 48,000 fans to the Cotton Bowl for a home opener against Navy. The Mustangs played most of their home games in the Cotton Bowl.

He truly was BMOC, Big Man on Campus. Even school President Willis Tate jumped on the bandwagon, joking at a campus fundraising drive that the school was to be renamed Southern Meredith University.

"SMU Renamed by Grid Hero," the student newspaper headlined.

In a letter to Meredith, Tate congratulated him for his selection as team captain. "On every hand I hear praise for you and the way you conduct yourself. Your high sense of values has made your influence a worthy one, and we at the university are grateful for what you are."

Meredith took one last part of SMU home with him. He married Alma Lynne Shamburger, described in press accounts as "a bright and gracious campus beauty queen." She was the daughter of a Texas oil millionaire from Wichita Falls. Meredith and his bride had a daughter, Mary.

College was fun, but now Meredith was about to enter a world in which his fame would grow a hundredfold—the

SMU Renamed By Grid Hero

Name's no longer the same!

President Willis Tate announced at the sustentation drive Sunday that the name of Southern Methodist University has been changed to Southern Meredith University.

The reason for this sudden change can be credited to the Mustangs sparkling quarterback Don Meredith, who has led the Ponies to wins in the last two conference games and has made them prospects for a possible post-season bowl bid.

The Dallas Morning News agreed with President Tate, for they bannered this new title in the sport's section of Monday's paper.

This appeared in *The Daily Campus*, the student newspaper at SMU.

National Football League. But forming a team to challenge tough veterans was no easy task.

Meredith used unorthodox means to get there, as did the big-time team owners.

CHAPTER 5

PERSONAL SERVICES CONTRACT

U PON HIS college graduation in 1959 with a bachelor's degree in business administration, Don Meredith could not believe his good fortune.

Dallas millionaire Clint Murchison Jr. was fighting to bring an NFL team to Dallas. It was called the Dallas Rangers, but that wouldn't last because a minor league baseball team already had the name.

Murchison (pronounced Murkison) thought he could count on Meredith putting fans in seats.

Meredith, John Eisenberg writes in *Ten-Gallon War: The NFL's Cowboys, the AFL's Texans, and the Feud for Dallas's Pro Football Future*, "was tall and rangy, possessed an accurate arm and also was articulate and light hearted, a fun young man who could charm a crowd and sell tickets. His sparkling blue eyes and bright smile lit his long, angular face."

To lock him into taking the quarterback job if a team ever materialized, Murchison, the son of one of America's most successful oilmen, offered Meredith an unorthodox five-year "personal services" contract for a stunning $150,000—$1.6 million in today's dollars.

Picture that: such a sum going to an East Texas high school sports hero and college All-American who had never played a second of pro football. One football writer called the offer "astonishing," especially for an unproven rookie. But before it could come into play, Murchison had to convince the other owners that Dallas should be in their exclusive club.

In a 2009 profile, *Dallas Morning News* sportswriter Brad Townsend noted that Meredith, then just 21, signed to play for a proposed NFL team that had no nickname, no coach and no other players.

In return, Meredith was promised that eventually he would be the starting quarterback. Or, if the NFL didn't greenlight the team, Meredith would work for one of Murchison's companies. But Meredith had another plan: "I'm either going to be an NFL quarterback, or I'm going to law school."

Actually, Chicago Bears owner George Halas selected Meredith in the third round of the draft the Cowboys missed because they weren't an official team yet. But in a prearranged deal, he traded him to Murchison in return for draft picks.

Murchison benefited from a competing American Football League team, the Dallas Texans. NFL owners didn't want an AFL competitor to gain a head start in Dallas.

To stop that from happening, the owners accepted Murchison's proposed team. Quickly, the name was changed.

Hello, Dallas Cowboys.

When Meredith signed that first contract on Nov. 28, 1959, the Mount Vernon star joined the team even before head coach/football genius Tom Landry was hired.

Dandy Don Meredith *is* the first Dallas Cowboy.

CHAPTER 6

THE FIGHT FOR A TEAM

MURCHISON FACED three obstacles: the NFL owners, whom he eventually won over; a reluctant fan base obsessed with high school and college football; and the competing Dallas Texans owned by Lamar Hunt, son of another legendary Texas oilman, H.L. Hunt. The Texans were a member of the upstart American Football League.

Fan apathy for pro football in Dallas was strong. Back in the early 1950s, the city had a professional NFL team, the Dallas Texans. But nobody cared, and it shut down after one season.

In 1960, Dallas suddenly had two pro teams, both owned by sons of ultra-wealthy oil men.

When Lamar Hunt asked to buy into the NFL with his proposed team, the Dallas Texans, he was denied. He responded with one of the boldest moves in the history of professional sports: He formed his own league, the American Football League, with headquarters in Dallas.

The AFL was announced in August 1959 with eight teams: the New York Titans (later Jets), Houston Oilers, Denver Broncos, Boston Patriots, Buffalo Bills, Oakland Raiders, Los Angeles Chargers and Dallas Texans.

From the beginning, the Texans and fledgling Cowboys had an intense rivalry. Starting in the 1960 season both teams played home games in the Cotton Bowl and wooed the same fans.

Their conflict mirrored the bigger battle between the historic NFL and the cocky AFL, which had sued the older league for antitrust violations and lost. Nationally and locally, the two leagues fought for players and attention.

To borrow a cliché: Dallas wasn't big enough for both of them.

Even an AFL championship couldn't save Hunt's team. In 1962 the Dallas Texans beat the Houston Oilers and took the title. But the team still wasn't profitable. Something had to give.

Photo taken Feb. 8, 1960, shortly after the Cowboys are admitted into the NFL. From left, Cowboys founder and owner Clint Murchison Jr., coach Tom Landry, Meredith and early investor Bedford Wynne.

CHAPTER 7

FOR A SONG

YOU KNOW the expression that something is sold so cheaply it went *for a song*?

In this story, there might not be a Dallas Cowboys if it weren't for a song.

George Preston Marshall, owner of the Washington Redskins (now Commanders), blocked the Cowboys entry into the NFL. The reasons were purely selfish. For decades, Redskins games were broadcast throughout the South. Another Southern team would cut into that.

For the Redskins' fight song, Marshall's wife, Corinne, wrote the lyrics and band leader Barney Briskin wrote the music. Marshall was super proud of his halftime show, and the fight song was a key element.

Hail to the Redskins!
Hail Victory!
Braves on the warpath!
Fight for old D.C.!

Corrine divorced her husband, who also fired Briskin, the band leader. The aggrieved pair decided on a payback. They sold Murchison the rights to their song. What happened next has two versions. In one, Murchison confronted Marshall by phone. In the other, he confronted Marshall face to face at the NFL owners meeting.

Murchison began by asking Marshall, "Does the Redskins band intend to play the Redskins fight song?"

"They sure will," Marshall answered.

"The heck they will," Murchison responded. "Nobody plays my fight song without my permission."

Marshall, now remembered as the last NFL owner to integrate his team, couldn't imagine games without his beloved song. Murchison went in for the kill.

"You'll never play that song again. And there's now a restraining order. Halftime shows are over. You're done unless you want to rethink the Cowboys vote."

Marshall relented. The trade was made. That's how the Cowboys were created. That's how their owner made it happen *for a song*.

CHAPTER 8

KANSAS CITY, HERE WE COME

Even though the Dallas Texans captured the AFL championship in 1962, Hunt gained a victory but lost the overall conflict. With meager attendance (at least four games under 20,000), he couldn't make any money.

The mayor of Kansas City offered him the ultimate deal: Kansas City would guarantee the sale of 25,000 season tickets, provide use of Municipal Stadium (Cotton Bowl rental was expensive), expand the stadium to 45,000 seats and provide offices and a training facility for free. The team also would get half of the concessions; it received none in Dallas.

Hunt met with Murchison.

"Look, this really isn't working," Hunt told him. "One of us needs to leave. We'll pay you to go."

"We don't want to leave," Murchison answered. "We aren't leaving."

"Well, then pay us to leave," Hunt said.

Murchison agreed, paying around $300,000 in a "farewell fee."

The Kansas City Chiefs were born. Suddenly, Dallas was a one-team town.

In June 1966, the American Football League and the National Football League announced a historic merger. Four years later, by the 1970 season, they officially combined to form one league with two conferences, the NFC and the AFC.

THE ORIGINAL TRIPLETS

ALL COWBOYS fans (and foes) know the "Triplets" who led the Cowboys to three Super Bowl victories in the early 1990s. QB Troy Aikman, running back Emmitt Smith and wide receiver Michael Irvin are all Hall of Famers.

But here are the original triplets put together by team owner Murchison. They would be with Meredith his entire playing career and lay the foundation to build a dynasty as "America's Team."

Murchison hired Tex Schramm as general manager. Schramm had served as Los Angeles Rams GM before quitting to be an assistant sports director for CBS.

Back in football, one of Schramm's first tasks was to hire Tom Landry as head coach, a decision that eventually elevated Landry to one of football's greatest. A former player-coach for the Giants, Landry previously worked as the Giants defensive coordinator. Another future legend, Vince Lombardi, was the Giants offensive coordinator. Landry moved back to Dallas, where he kept a home, and Lombardi would make history in Green Bay as the new Packers coach. Their paths would cross in some of the NFL's greatest games.

Schramm hired Gil Brandt as scouting director, and Brandt would change scouting for pro sports teams in a big way. The Cowboys were the first team to build a system using computers and psychological tests in search of players. When Brandt showed up at an NFL draft with a bulky computer and accessories, other teams' executives laughed at him. That mocking didn't last when he found sleeper players, overlooked by competitors, often at historically Black colleges and universities.

After Meredith was hired, University of New Mexico running back Don Perkins also signed a personal services contract. Perkins, the first Black player on the team, was actually the only bright spot. He missed the first season with a broken foot, but by 1961 the rookie was one of the best running backs in the league.

These original triplets, Schramm, Landry and Brandt, kept their jobs from 1960 until 1989 when a guy from Arkansas who shall remain nameless bought the Cowboys and removed all three.

The original Cowboys Brain Trust meeting in 1986 at
Valley Ranch. From left, Gil Brandt, Tom Landry and Tex Schramm.

CHAPTER 10

NOBODY'S TEAM

Long before the Dallas Cowboys became America's team, before they became the top-valued sports franchise in the world worth almost $9 billion, before their TV ratings became the highest of any sport, they were nobody's team.

In their 1960 debut tickets were less than $5. Free tickets were available through promotions, but even so, the Cotton Bowl was mostly empty. Attendance hosting the San Francisco 49ers was listed as 10,000. At the time, the Cotton Bowl seated 75,000.

It didn't help that in that first season, the Cowboys didn't win a single game. The expansion team was composed of unprotected cast-offs from other teams, including past-their-prime veterans, mediocre journeymen and rookies hardly anyone noticed. They had no players because the Cowboys were not allowed in the NFL draft as they were not yet approved.

Entering a nearly empty stadium for one game, Meredith cracked, "Well, we finally did it. We scared everyone off."

Aside from seeing all of those empty seats, Meredith heard something else when he entered the Cotton Bowl.

Boooooo!!!

"I had never even really heard that," he explained.

Booooooo!!!

He had better get used to it. For most of his career, Meredith would serve as a favorite target for some journalists who promoted the image of a playboy quarterback who didn't properly prepare for games and didn't take his job as seriously as he should.

The Dallas Cowboys play the New York Giants on Dec. 1, 1963.
Notice all the empty seats at the Cotton Bowl.

A program from the earliest days of the Cowboys, August 1960.

CHAPTER 11

MADDENING SWIRL

ROOKIE MEREDITH, the classic mythical hero, did not start in those early days. Coach Landry said the timetable to develop into a pro quarterback was around five years. Meredith didn't want to wait that long. His king-sized contract with little payoff for the fans hung over him like a dark cloud.

From that day in 1960 when he first stepped on the field, no one could know how he would carve the template for what would become one of the most storied figures in professional sports—Dallas Cowboys quarterback.

Think Staubach, Morton, Aikman, Romo, Prescott.

So well known, they go by one name only.

As writer John Eisenberg notes in his memoir, *Cotton Bowl Days: Growing Up with Dallas and the Cowboys in the 1960s*, Meredith represented the beginning of pro sports in Dallas. "The maddening swirl that exists today—four major sports teams and dozens of prominent personalities, the endless controversies and overlapping seasons, the shouting on the radio and bluster in the newspapers, the money and the opinions flying everywhere—all traces back to one Joseph Donald Meredith.

"He was the first Dallas athlete to hear venomous criticism, the first whose salary was an issue, the first whose personality became as relevant to fans as his performance.... Meredith was years before his time."

Meredith plays for Landry for a decade, but the pair never get along. They are too different.

CHAPTER 12

ROOKIE DEBUT

WHEN LANDRY and Meredith sat down to talk plays, it was clear to Landry that the freewheeling college QB wasn't interested in the game's complexities. He only wanted to run, throw and score.

Contrast the coach's methodical system with his new quarterback's play-for-the-moment approach.

This was something of a surprise to Landry, so he acted fast. Eddie LeBaron, the 5-foot-7, former longtime Redskins QB, had earned his law degree in the off-season and retired from football to practice law. But he got a pitch from Schramm: Come be the Cowboys' starting QB and also mentor young Meredith. LeBaron wanted to play for Landry, so he agreed.

This expansion team resembled another legendary expansion franchise of that era—baseball's 1962 New York Mets, known for their mistakes and their ability to lose 100 games their first season.

In one game against Baltimore that inaugural 1960 season, LeBaron threw three completions to his teammates and three to the Colts. The following week, Meredith was summoned from the bench to start against the Los Angeles Rams. "Ordinarily it takes three years for a rookie to develop, but I believe this boy can do it in one." Out of desperation perhaps, Landry kept shortening the timeline rookie quarterbacks needed to start in the NFL.

Against the Rams, Meredith missed 10 passes in a row and threw three interceptions. A flop.

Privately, Meredith complained about his lack of playing time, and it set the tone for his relationship with Landry.

Eddie LeBaron, all 5-foot, 7-inches of him, comes out of retirement to play for Landry and mentor Meredith, who later says LeBaron taught him more about being a quarterback than Landry ever did.

"It was two years before Landry even spoke to me," he said. "I learned more from Eddie than I did from Landry."

The New York Times reported that Meredith didn't like his coach's pregame homework and that he "favored his own wits over Landry's playbook."

Meredith's totals for season one: He played in six games, completing only 29 of 68 passes for 42% (lowest of his career) with five interceptions and two touchdowns. The Cowboys finished 0-11-1, with the highlight a tie with the New York Giants. "It was like we had won the world championship," one player recalled.

CHAPTER 13

I'LL GET BETTER

FOR THE INITIAL home game in Dallas before 30,000 people at the Cotton Bowl, Tex Schramm hired Roy Rogers and his wife, Dale Evans, two top cowboy movie stars, to sit in a convertible and smile and wave while making one lap around the field. But spectators began pelting the couple with ice cubes, paper cups and programs. When Rogers stood up and angrily yelled at them, Cowboys officials cut the ride short.

And so it went that first season.

Landry was in no hurry to play Meredith. Denne Freeman and Jaime Aron, authors of *I Remember Tom Landry*, write that "Don had that gunslinger mentality and wanted to throw the bomb. Tom wanted him to read defenses."

LeBaron played most of the time. When Meredith played, he was shaky. Both were sacked a lot because the offensive line was beyond bad. Gary Cartwright wrote in *Sport* magazine that "in the early years, the offensive line had been a bunch of little guys with bells on their toes and feathers in their caps, strumming banjos, talking to geese, and occasionally inquiring about the health of their quarterback."

Landry wanted to get Meredith playing time because he was the hometown boy with the SMU following.

Offensive lineman Mike Connelly recalled that Meredith "was just such a clown all the time, and that's what caused trouble. Tom bent over backwards. He was so patient with Dandy, but he hated that he had to wait for him to get serious because he would come in and wouldn't know the audibles. He'd look at us in the huddle and sing his songs. He wouldn't know what was going on out there. He'd call an audible, but he'd call the wrong one."

One night in Detroit, Meredith stayed up partying. He was certain he wasn't going to play, but on game day Landry came over and told him he was going to start. Meredith was so surprised that he forgot to put on his uniform pants and had to be reminded before he left the locker room. Probably word got back to Landry; regardless, Meredith didn't start.

Another time Landry sent in a play, but Meredith sketched out his own play on the grass and scored a touchdown with it. Returning to the sidelines triumphant, Meredith was chewed out by Landry for not following the game plan.

When he finally got that first start against the Rams, Meredith played poorly and knew it. "I looked bad today. I have a long way to go and a lot to learn. There are bound to be days like this. I'll get better."

True that.

Benched again, he pouted. "I was really immature," he told the *Los Angeles Times* in 1966. "I got that five-year contract, and I thought I was something. When Landry put me on the bench, I thought I would hurt him by not working. I just hurt myself."

CHAPTER 14

BOO!

"AND BOOING?" asked Meredith's high school football and basketball coach, Wayne Pierce. "In Mount Vernon you don't boo anybody. They'd get you right out of there if you did."

At first Meredith said he didn't care, but the criticism did wear on him, and he went into a funk.

Booing Meredith became a Dallas thing.

Blackie Sherrod: "No one was questioning his physical ability, his strong, whippy arm, his agility, his courage. It was those untimely interceptions, fumbles, busted signals and such. The long bombs from his quick arm, the desperate scrambling he did to preserve limb if not life, were ignored by the critics. Their judgment was based on the scoreboard of major opponents."

CHAPTER 15

THE QB SHUFFLE

IN A QUANDARY, Landry began alternating LeBaron and Meredith on every down. Meredith disliked the idea, but it worked for LeBaron who said, "If you were the first and third down quarterback, you got to throw a lot. If you were the second down quarterback, you didn't."

LeBaron retired after the 1963 season, and Meredith started most games in 1964, but he didn't always get to finish. He endured the QB shuffle with two rookies—Jerry Rhome and Craig Morton. When he played poorly, he was benched again.

Wide receiver Frank Clarke said, "Tom kept changing quarterbacks, and it was definitely chaotic."

Hall of Fame defensive tackle Bob Lilly, the first player drafted by the Cowboys, once said he hated the quarterback shuffle. "The quarterback could never get in sync, and we knew that as players."

When Landry gave his problem QB a start on Halloween 1965 against the Pittsburgh Steelers, Meredith responded by completing only 12 of 34 passes. He fumbled twice. He threw a pass for a touchdown, but it was nullified because he had crossed the line of scrimmage. He fumbled a snap as a holder for the field goal kicker. Another touchdown pass was called back for a penalty. He stepped out of bounds a foot shy of a first down. The Cowboys lost 22-13, their fifth straight defeat.

For much of his career, Meredith doesn't get great protection from his offensive line.

Tight end Pettis Norman said in his book, *The Pettis Norman Story,* that Meredith lost self-confidence and that Landry benching him really affected the confidence of the team.

Defensive coordinator Dick Nolan said in an oral history, *Cowboys Have Always Been My Heroes* by Peter Golenbock, that Meredith was very emotional and would have enjoyed having Landry as a friend. "Don would have liked to have Tom say, 'Hey Don, you did a great job,' and pat him on the back. But that was not Tom. He was not that way."

Landry's way was not to praise a Cowboy player for making an interception. That was the player's job.

After that Steelers loss, Landry locked the locker room for a team meeting. He spoke. He coughed. Then he cried, saying, "I very likely won't be here next year." Considering that his stoic expression rarely changed, this was a once-in-a-lifetime experience for his players. He made a confession:

"I've never been ashamed of you before, but I am now. I know what you can do. I know what you're capable of doing. The people that beat you today don't have any business being on the same field with you. What's the excuse for it? There are no excuses.

"Who's at fault? There are too many faults, too many mistakes, so I realize now whose fault it is. It must be mine. I'm the one who lets you down, and I want you to tell me how and where. There's no other explanation for what happened to us, that's kept us from being a team playing as a team. I don't know what else to say."

Silence. Then Meredith stood up. "I can only talk for myself," he said. "I've tried to do my best, and I haven't done it. I've let myself down, I know. What hurts me is I've let everybody else down, when you depended on me. I know I can play better, but I ain't going to promise that. I thought I was trying hard, but now I'm going to try harder. That's what I promise you—there won't be a man on this team who'll devote himself more to making us what we ought to be, and we're going to be."

Landry said in that meeting that he would not play Meredith the rest of the season. What followed was a QB controversy, not only with fans, but with the offensive team. According to *The Last Cowboy: A Life of Tom Landry* by Mark Ribowsky, Landry called the 48 hours after the Steelers loss "two of the worst days of my coaching career." Everyone—public and press alike—had turned on Meredith, with good reason.

"I tossed and turned for two miserable nights," the coach said. "I prayed for wisdom to make the right choice."

Before he made his decision public, Landry met with Meredith, who expected the worst. His career as a Cowboy might be over. He was "ready for the blow he knew had to be coming," Landry recalled. But it did not come.

"Don, I believe in you," Landry said to his listener's surprise. "You're my starting quarterback for the rest of the year." Meredith cried, and Landry joined him.

He made the announcement at a press conference. "We need a quarterback to lift us to our potential, and that is why I have made this decision."

Dallas was 2-5 halfway through the season after five consecutive losses, but with their singing QB, the Cowboys won five of the final seven games and finished in a tie for second place in the Eastern Conference with the New York Giants, four games behind the defending NFL champion Cleveland Browns (11-3).

Landry would describe sticking with Meredith as one of the toughest decisions of his career. It turned out to be right.

CHAPTER 16

THE LOST YEARS

THOSE EARLY seasons, 1960-1964, were lost years for the Cowboys and especially Meredith. He was battered and bruised physically, mentally and emotionally. Looking back on 1961, he said he became "rebellious and antagonistic" about the situation. "I really thought Tom was wrong, and it became sort of a personal thing, which was the worst thing which could have happened to me. I wasn't hurting him, just myself."

But things were about to change. In 1965, the Cowboys unleashed a new weapon who would change pro football and the rules by which it is played.

His name was Bob Hayes.

CHAPTER 17

BULLET BOB

"BULLET" BOB HAYES was the world's fastest human. He earned that title by winning the 1964 Olympics 100-meter dash in a record time of 10 seconds. But could he play professional football? The Cowboys signed him, so they'd soon find out.

"As days went by in my first Cowboys training camp, I started to make an impression on the veteran players," Hayes wrote in his autobiography, *Run, Bullet, Run: The Rise, Fall, and Recovery of Bob Hayes.* "Meredith and I became friends when he learned that I could catch the ball, and I discovered that when he went back and cocked his arm and threw, the ball would be where it was supposed to be."

In the 1965 home opener against the New York Giants, Hayes' first professional game, he caught touchdown passes for 74 and 39 yards. Suddenly, the QB and his new receiver were destroying NFL defenses. Suddenly, the stadium announcer had a new line: "Meredith to Bob Hayes for the touchdown!" Final score in Hayes' debut: 31-2, Dallas. The following week, Dallas beat the Redskins 27-7 on three long passes to Hayes.

Olympic gold medalist Bob Hayes is officially "the world's fastest man."
Defenders cannot keep up with the Cowboys wide receiver. With Don Meredith's
accurate passing, he and Hayes form a strong scoring partnership.

NFL coaches, long dependent on man-to-man coverage, didn't know what to do. At first they double teamed him, but they couldn't catch him. Wide receiver Frank Clarke told author Golenbock, "We were all quite stunned watching him run. It was really a tribute to Don Meredith how quickly Don got to where he could get Bob Hayes the ball. He didn't underthrow Bob very much, and we were very impressed with how quickly Dandy was able to do that. One of the things that helped: Bob Hayes and Meredith practiced a lot after our regular practice. They spent a lot of time together."

The NFL changed the rules to let defensive players "bump" receivers at the line of scrimmage to slow them down. NFL teams also turned to the zone defense against Hayes. "He changed the game," said defensive lineman Larry Cole, who played in five Cowboys Super Bowls.

Before that 1965 season, the Cowboys in five years had never won more games than they lost. finished. They were 4-9-1 in 1961, 5-8-1 in 1962, 4-10 in 1963, 5-8-1 in 1964.

In '65 the team had its first .500 season with a 7-7 record. With Meredith at quarterback the team won five of its last seven games.

CHAPTER 18

CONTRACT EXTENDED

MEREDITH NEEDED football as a distraction from his personal life. He divorced Lynne before the 1963 season. They remarried at the end of the season but broke up again, and Lynne and their daughter moved out of state. Meredith missed his daughter terribly.

Even with Hayes added to his receiver arsenal, Meredith, often playing through injuries, struggled in the 1965 season. Against the Redskins he was only 6-25 passing. Against the St. Louis Cardinals he went 9-25. On one play he missed a wide-open Hayes in the end zone. After the Cowboys lost 20-13, Landry made a move. Ribowsky writes in *The Last Cowboy*: "On the plane home, he told a reporter, 'I'm going to have to make a decision about Meredith. We can't go on without a passing game.'"

Wide receiver Buddy Dial explained that Meredith felt anguish, but he "didn't want to hurt anybody or get even. All he wanted to do was win, and that's a class act. He just kept it to himself."

Officially, it was the 1965 season—Meredith's sixth—where Landry designated him, once and for all time the starting quarterback. "Hey, the guy has shown me a lot," Landry said.

Landry heard fans' booing, too. He knew some of it was for him. Murchison responded to critics in 1964 by signing Landry to an unheard of 10-year contract extension.

Schramm worked on a new contact for Meredith and completely disregarded 1964, saying, "His performance was poor because of circumstances. He was injured before the season started and it got worse with each game. But he continued to play when most players would have quit. He has the deepest respect and admiration from our entire organization."

Meredith extended his contract for another five years. "I got what I wanted, and I hope the club gets what it wanted."

CHAPTER 19

JFK

THE WORST DAY for the Cowboys, for the fans, for the city and, to that date, for America came on Nov. 22, 1963. When President John F. Kennedy was assassinated in Dallas, much of the world went into mourning. NFL Commissioner Pete Rozelle made a grave mistake ordering the NFL to continue its regular season games.

Big D got a new nickname—"City of Hate." Bob Lilly, one of the team's best players, told Eisenberg that Dallas had been "kind of a coming star" and suddenly it was tarnished. "It took Dallas a long time to get over it, of course. It didn't take the team quite as long. Meredith and I, as Texans, probably felt it a little more. Coach Landry, too. We were kind of ashamed of our city. It's not the best mentality for playing football."

Pettis Norman, the longtime tight end, wrote in his autobiography that "sadness and gloom came over the team."

Two days after the assassination, the Cowboys had to play the Browns in Cleveland. It was the same day Jack Ruby shot and killed Lee Harvey Oswald in front of the world. The stadium public address announcer didn't say Dallas Cowboys, just the Cowboys.

The Cowboys didn't have their hearts in the game and fell 27-17. Meredith threw two interceptions that were turned into touchdowns. He finished 13-30, no TDs and four interceptions.

Still to come, 1966 would be a big year.

CHAPTER 20

RACISM, DALLAS STYLE

YOU CAN'T recount the early history of the Dallas Cowboys without examining a contentious and embarrassing issue that bedeviled the team—and also Meredith's role as team leader.

White players lived in North Dallas, close to team training facilities. Black players had to live in or around Oak Cliff. This added an extra 20 minutes to the drive.

Bob Hayes recalled how when he joined the team, white players weren't allowed to room with Black players. He said no such limitations existed on the U.S. Olympic team.

"If we wanted to go out at night, the Blacks and the whites lived too far apart to go out together. So the team split into white and Black cliques."

In 1962 not one Dallas hotel welcomed Black players from visiting teams. Schramm lobbied white business leaders for help and convinced the Ramada Inn near Love Field to integrate. But there was a condition. Other hotels couldn't spread the word because that could lead to a boycott of Ramada.

Dallas had a restaurant problem, too. Black players had a difficult time finding places to eat. They couldn't even stand on the street without police hassling them.

Away games, especially in the South, were troublesome. Once, in New Orleans, Hayes noticed a homemade banner near the top of the stadium showing Meredith and him (identified by their jersey numbers) with nooses around their necks. The Saints organization wouldn't take the banner down.

Wide receiver Frank Clarke, one of the first Black Cowboys, recalled: "You could walk into a 5-and-10 cent store and see drinking fountains marked 'Colored' and 'White.' I had never seen this. It kind of takes your breath away. You go, 'Holy smokes. How far away are we from lynchings?' Though we didn't have any cause to be threatened, I could not divorce myself from the fact we were in Texas."

Don Perkins recalled being invited to lunch with Gil Brandt and Meredith at Highland Park Cafeteria. A waiter walked up to Perkins and said, "Hey, you can't get served here." The group walked out.

Perkins called a real estate agent about a listed apartment vacancy, but once they met, the agent said the apartment had already been rented.

"It's not easy for a Negro athlete to live in Texas," Perkins complained to a reporter back home in New Mexico where he lived with his family in the off-season. "The Negroes on the Cowboys can only find roach-infested houses. Right now, I don't have a place to stay for this season. If I don't find something soon, I'll be camping on Tex Schramm's doorstep. I think he should know of the places that have been offered to us, and also the places where we have been refused."

Schramm told reporter Steve Perkins that Don Perkins (no relation) didn't have to camp outside. "He can move into my house with me."

Addressing "the Negro problem," Schramm gave his take: There were problems in housing in Dallas and in jobs and schools. "The same is true all over. It's not something unique to the Cowboys."

He added, "I wish he'd [Perkins] kept his mouth shut until he got to training camp."

Then Schramm added: "Who integrated Dallas hotels? We did, when we brought in NFL teams. Who started integrated seating in Dallas? We did, in the Cotton Bowl, and nobody even noticed it…. But we're ending segregation. Can anybody name another line of work, another profession, where skin color doesn't mean anything?"

Schramm was meeting with apartment owners and had eliminated the roommate rules. From now on, rookies would be assigned roommates based on alphabetical order and not skin color.

Landry addressed the issue with his team, saying: "Fellas, we know what's going on here. We don't particularly agree with it, but that's the way it is, so we have to do what we can do, so we don't create unnecessary problems."

It all sounded good, but it was hardly enough. Segregation, although illegal, was rampant. In Dallas the method whites used to keep Blacks out of neighborhoods was firebombing their homes. It was a terrifying time for Black families.

Gratitude goes to future Hall of Fame defensive back Mel Renfro for making a difference.

His father warned him not to get involved, saying, "Melvin, don't make a scene. It will only cause you trouble."

Renfro didn't follow that advice. He and his wife, Pat, tried for two years to find a place in North Dallas. In one case, an apartment manager told them over the phone that they could rent a place for $350 a month. When Pat went to set it up, she was told the apartment was now up for sale and not a rental.

Mel Renfro is one of the heroes of the early Cowboys. Not only is he
an amazing player, but he takes on the segregated housing market in
Dallas in a federal lawsuit — and wins!

"I was so upset I could hardly play the game," Renfro wrote
in his autobiography, *Forever a Cowboy*. "I later shared with
my teammates what had happened. They weren't surprised
by it. Many of the Black players admitted they had experienced the same thing themselves."

After the assassination of the Rev. Martin Luther King Jr.,
Congress passed and President Lyndon B. Johnson signed the
Fair Housing Act of 1968, which prohibited discrimination

concerning the sale, rental and financing of housing based on race, religion, national origin or gender.

Dallas lawyer and former state Senator Oscar Holcombe Mauzy heard about Renfro's problems.

He called Renfro: "Mel, do you want to fight this?"

"You bet I do," Renfro replied.

"I'll represent you for free."

They filed the first civil rights suit in a Texas federal court under the new housing law.

When the Cowboys learned Renfro was taking the matter to court, Schramm called Renfro into his office where "for 35 to 40 minutes he hammered me."

"Mel, you can't do this! This is going to hurt you."

"But I've been hurt by being denied housing," Renfro replied.

Mauzy petitioned the court to allow the Renfros to move into the Executive Duplex Apartments in North Dallas.

Opposing lawyers badgered Renfro, and some real estate people tried to block the case, fearing it would turn the Dallas real estate market upside down.

Sarah T. Hughes, the federal judge who swore Johnson in as president on the plane after the Kennedy assassination, presided over the case.

Renfro won the case, along with $1,500 in damages. The apartment complex owner told him he could have his pick of any vacant duplex. But because the address was well known and Renfro feared for his family's safety, they took another apartment in the neighborhood.

Renfro always believed that Schramm punished him by paying a lesser salary than other players in the league who played the same position.

Renfro played in 10 consecutive Pro Bowls and four Super Bowls. But his biggest victory almost surely came in the courtroom.

As for Meredith's role in healing racial wounds, Bob Hayes wrote in his autobiography, "Even though Don was one of those good old boys from East Texas and SMU, he was fair to everyone on the team, not just to the white guys. I would say that the Black guys felt more comfortable around Meredith than we did around any other white players on the team.

"The bottom line was that we won with Meredith. We were happy with Meredith. We were comfortable with Meredith, and Meredith was a leader on the team. He may not have been the all-out serious leader. But leadership is leadership."

Star fullback Walt Garrison agreed: "When Meredith was with the Cowboys the locker-room atmosphere was always great. The team spirit, the camaraderie between the players, Blacks and whites, was the best....

"Most of that was due to Joe Don. He was the undisputed team leader. And just because of the way he was—friendly, up front, easygoing and fun—we were always a happy team.

"After practice we'd go down to the beer joint and work out any problems we had. Meredith set that up. Thursday afternoon was officially 'Beer Joint Day' because that was the last day of hard practice for the week. And most of the team would go down to the VIP Lounge, a bar off the Central Expressway. Meredith would get up and sing and drink and talk and drink and just generally hold court. 'OK, what's wrong? Who's got a beef?'"

CHAPTER 21

GOLDEN HELMET

IN HIS AUTOBIOGRAPHY, Pettis Norman, who is Black, writes, "I began thinking about the rent I paid while leasing apartments. I looked at the quality of housing available. Then it dawned on me that I should build an apartment complex and become a landlord of affordable, quality apartments.

"With what became approximately a half-million-dollar loan—an extraordinary amount of money back then—I worked with architects, engineers, and construction companies to build 74 units in South Dallas."

He named them the Golden Helmet Apartments and opened them with great pride. The Golden Helmet still exists today, operating under a new name.

Pettis Norman, foreground, celebrates the opening of his housing
complex in Dallas. He built the Golden Helmet Apartments,
which still exist today under a different name.
Joining him at the event is Mel Renfro.

BUBBLES CASH

THE STORY of the Dallas Cowboys' first decade cannot be told without Bubbles Cash, a stripper who danced at Jack Ruby's Carousel Club, among other places. Bubbles' story is not necessarily about football as much as it reflects the culture of the times.

Bubbles' real name was Esemay, and her last name was actually Cash. She supposedly got the nickname as a child blowing bubbles. But is there a better name than Bubbles Cash? For a stripper?

It was the 1967 season when the Cowboys were playing Atlanta in the Cotton Bowl. After the game began, she walked down the aisle in her white high heels at the 50-yard line behind the Cowboys' bench. As Eisenberg tells it in *Cotton Bowl Days*, "her blonde hair was piled atop her head. She wore a tight sweater and a leopard-skin mini-skirt. She carried two helpings of pink cotton candy, which she held at chest level."

First, a few fans shouted encouragement. Some whistled. Then the outburst grew. Such a commotion arose in the stands that the players looked up to see what the fuss was about.

Dallas stripper Bubbles Cash is the Cowboys' unofficial mascot. When she makes her appearance on the 50-yard line in the first quarter of a game, all heads turn, even players'.

Bob Hayes told Meredith, "Dandy, look there!"

Meredith looked, then immediately called a timeout. As Hayes recalled, "Landry was on the sideline looking at us, and Meredith was looking right over Landry's head. So Landry thought Meredith was looking at him. But the quarterback did not jog over to the coach during the timeout to get his instructions. All of a sudden Landry turned around and saw Bubbles. Then he turned back to Meredith, who had wasted one of three timeouts we got in each half."

Landry scolded: "What did you call timeout for?"

"Bubbles Cash, Coach."

Landry was speechless.

Dallas Morning News photographer Joe Laird took a classic picture. You can count at least 40 smiling faces.

There's more happiness in that moment than fans usually felt during those lost early years. Bubbles' trips down the aisle became a tradition at every home game and a few away games, too. Sometimes, the game would stop.

Walt Garrison recalls in *Once a Cowboy*, "She always waited for the middle of the first quarter to make her entrance. You knew she was coming when you heard the crowd start going, 'Aaahhh.'"

Bubbles became the Cowboys' unofficial mascot. Her photo appeared in the game program. She signed autographs with double B's like her first name and a dollar sign for her last name.

Get this: BB$ ran for governor of Texas—twice. Her slogans were "Texas needs Cash" and "Bet on Bubbles."

Why tell this story? According to Cowboys lore, Tex Schramm considered this phenomenon and declared, "We could sell this."

Not long after, teen boys and girls organized and started cheering on the sidelines. Called CowBelles & Beaux, the group lasted a few years. When the boys were given their walking papers, some of the girls stayed on. Schramm called in Dee Brock, considered the creator of the modern Cowboys Cheerleaders. The cheerleaders quickly gained fame, known across the land for their hot pants, halter tops and white leather go-go boots.

It's not much of a stretch to draw a line from BB$ to Schramm's "We could sell this" to the world-famous Cowboys Cheerleaders.

Sarah Hepola, who created a documentary about the cheerleaders called "America's Girls," declared that the day BB$ walked down the center aisle for the first time was the day "the sexual revolution arrived in Dallas."

If true, Coach Landry was not a fan. The authors of *I Remember Tom Landry* wrote, "The only time Landry and Schramm came close to clashing was over the cheerleaders. Landry didn't like the idea of their sideline gyrations stirring up fans."

Schramm said, "Tom was very cold to it, saying it was something he didn't approve of. Then one time he referred to them as 'porno queens.'"

Schramm asked Landry to come to his office. "I told Tom we had a difference of philosophy, and I knew how he felt, but to call the cheerleaders 'porno queens' was a bad thing."

Schramm had an actual porn video and popped it into a machine.

"This is what your name for them meant. Here is a girl without clothes. This is a real porn movie. Do you know what you were saying? There is a big difference."

Landry stood and walked out the door. He never mentioned the cheerleaders again.

BRAIN TRUST— GIL BRANDT

THE FRONT office executives who ran the Dallas Cowboys for three decades, the men who bet their careers on Meredith as QB, are fascinating in their own ways.

Gil Brandt, vice president of player personnel, often was described as a baby photographer in Milwaukee before he went into football scouting. But that's not true. He never took a photo. He gave cameras to nurses in maternity wards at three local hospitals with instructions on what to do.

According to his obituary, "He charmed nurses into taking photos of new arrivals in exchange for the hospital receiving part of the profits. He developed the photos in the basement of his parents' home, charging extra for the more modern photos in color."

Each hospital added $3 to the patient's bill and kept 75 cents. Brandt kept $2.25.

On the side, Brandt scouted for Schramm when Schramm was general manager of the Los Angeles Rams. He'd tell Schramm, "Hey, this guy is pretty good." He was usually right.

Gil Brandt

When Murchison hired Schramm to run the Cowboys, Schramm brought Brandt with him.

He was the ultimate pro football scout, responsible for more innovations than anyone else—ever. He knew the life story of obscure college prospects, their family members, their likes and dislikes, birthdays and anniversaries.

He courted prospects by sending players and coaches Cowboys T-shirts and other team souvenirs.

He sought not only good college football players but athletes from other sports—basketball, track and even soccer.

He also spent time getting to know athletes from the often overlooked Historically Black Colleges and Universities.

Brandt used a "black box" of flashing lights to test a player's reaction time, and he created the NFL scouting combine, which still exists and enables each team to test prospects on a range of skills.

Ever wonder why football coaches use the 40-yard dash to measure a player's acceleration? That was Brandt. He called 40 yards the best measurement for "football speed."

Brandt used psychological and intelligence testing, too. With Landry's plays so difficult to learn and remember, the team had no room for not-so-smart players.

Perhaps his main achievement was using computers to organize his draft picks. He'd lug his big computer to the draft. Other teams laughed. They had what they needed to know on index cards.

He maintained a sophisticated, for the times, software program that measured each prospect's talent plus the intangibles—character, competitiveness, strength, explosiveness, quickness, body control and mental alertness.

"They talk about analytics now," he told *The Wall Street Journal*. "We did the same thing 50 years ago, except we called it probabilities."

By 1963, his reliance on IBM computers was beginning to pay off. In the 1964 draft, the computer recommended track star Mel Renfro (second round), Bob Hayes (seventh round) and future QB Roger Staubach (10th round).

Brandt waited for a medical report on Renfro before making his pick. Since there were no time limits to announce picks back then, he waited eight hours, delaying the draft half a day.

Impatient, Lombardi called out, "What's the matter? Did your computer break?"

Gil Brandt was inducted into the Pro Football Hall of
Fame in 2019.

CHAPTER 24

BRAIN TRUST— TEX SCHRAMM

Texas Earnest Schramm was actually born in California.

He studied journalism at the University of Texas at Austin. After graduation he covered sports for the *Austin American-Statesman,* followed by PR work for the Rams, where he worked his way up to general manager.

He left football to be assistant sports director at CBS-TV, where he convinced reluctant executives to televise the 1960 Winter Olympics, the first time that happened. He brought news anchor Walter Cronkite to serve as sports anchor.

Murchison brought him in the minute Dallas became part of the NFL, and Schramm's first task was to hire a coach. Landry was his man.

Throughout his storied NFL career, Schramm was considered a vigorous negotiator, especially when it came to keeping player salaries down. "Some of you guys are getting too big for your britches," he'd say.

Tex Schramm

He was a key figure in the NFL-AFL merger. Some viewed him as the unofficial assistant commissioner because of the power he wielded.

He hired the first woman to run an NFL team's ticket office.

He pushed behind the scenes to get Dallas hotels to accept Black players from other teams.

As a member of the NFL's competition committee, he urged the league to align as two conferences with three divisions in each. He introduced wild-card games. He argued that instant replay would improve the game. He made sure the referees had microphones, so they could, in the words of one ref, "talk to America." He advocated for a 30-second play clock and fought for wind direction strips on goalposts.

He also made sure the Cowboys moved after one season into the Eastern Division even though they were located in the Southwest. Why? He wanted attention in the big media cities, New York, Philadelphia and Washington D.C.

In addition to creating the cheerleaders, he masterminded the building of Valley Ranch, the Cowboys' office and training complex with practice fields, team headquarters, a Cowboys retail store, player rooms and a TV studio.

No team in any sport had such a setup.

He and Meredith were close. They talked a lot. In a 1968 *Sports Illustrated* profile of Meredith by Bud Shrake, Schramm was especially candid about their relationship, and most of what he said was critical.

"Meredith has plenty of self-doubts," he told Shrake. "That's probably the reason for the finger-snapping façade he puts up. That façade is not his real nature.

"What Meredith should be is a singer or something where he can do what he wants to excel in without having to do the practice. Meredith doesn't enjoy practice. When the season starts, he'll work hard, but not in April. If he would work for three months in the spring throwing sideline passes to a receiver, there's little limit to what a great quarterback he would be. But Don resents any attempt to change him.

"When you've got your future riding on one guy, a quarterback, you like to have him be a little serious. You say, 'Be dedicated, pay the price.'… Sometimes I get annoyed at his flippancy.

"Last spring I told him he had to join the adult world. He got mad and stormed out of my office. The next day he came back and said, 'I'm not gonna join your adult world. I'll live in my world, and you live in yours.'

"He knows when he's not doing things right. He's tougher on himself than others are on him."

He was accessible in a way that a modern general manager would never be. Schramm kept his home phone number listed in the Dallas telephone book. Anyone could call at any time, and he'd answer.

Tex Schramm was inducted into the Pro Football Hall of Fame in 1991.

CHAPTER 25

BRAIN TRUST—
TOM LANDRY

AMERICA KNEW Tom Landry as the ultra-serious, stone-faced, formally dressed coach who always wore a fedora. They knew him as a strait-laced, deeply devout Christian who liked to sprinkle Bible verses when he talked football.

That truly was the man.

During a charity game in which the offense played the defense, Cornell Green intercepted a Meredith pass and was chased by Meredith who took off his helmet and waved it in the air as he galloped pretending he was riding a horse. Everyone laughed, except Landry who said: "Gentlemen, nothing funny ever happens on a football field—if we can help it."

Once, in 1979, in the middle of an embarrassing loss to Washington, linebacker Thomas "Hollywood" Henderson (he awarded himself that nickname) mugged for the camera on national television and showed off handkerchiefs with the team logo. Hollywood was dropped from the roster the next day.

Tom Landry

Landry and Meredith were complete opposites forced by circumstance to deal with each other in a nine-year-long soap opera steeped in drama. Author Ribowsky compared the pair to a bad comedy team: "Tom Landry playing a slow-burning, patronizing, and often cruel Abbott to Dandy Don's incorrigibly adolescent Costello."

Meredith would laugh at Landry when no one else dared.

"Aw, don't take me seriously," he told his coach, who only knew serious.

Like Meredith, Landry was a native Texan, growing up in the Rio Grande Valley. When he was working in New York for the Giants and his wife, Alicia, was pregnant, he made sure to get her home to Texas in time for the birth.

"Tommy laid down the law," she once explained. "They all had to be born in Texas. It was non-negotiable. It's a Texas thing."

When Landry was 20, he was co-piloting B-17s in World War II. He went on 30 bombing missions over Germany and Czechoslovakia. On one flight the engines cut out and the 11 crewmen were about to bail over enemy territory where they would surely be captured. But at the last moment, Landry tried the fuel knob one final time. The engines started up with such force that Landry was knocked backward. "We got power!" he shouted.

On another flight, the wings were sheared off from crash landing in a forest. Nobody was hurt. Ribowsky says the future football legend "cheated almost certain death."

After the war, Landry resumed his business studies at UT Austin. He also played defensive back and fullback on the football team. In the 1949 Orange Bowl Landry played every down on both sides, offense and defense, and his Longhorns beat Georgia in his final college game.

He played defensive back for the New York Giants for six years, then was a player-coach, then defensive coach. Vince Lombardi was the offensive coordinator. Their head coach, Jim Lee, handled the press and decided when to punt.

Lombardi left a year before Landry, giving Lombardi with his new Green Bay Packers team a one-year head start to coaching stardom.

When Schramm called Landry about coaching the Cowboys, Landry said he wanted to return to Dallas where he could continue to grow his insurance business during the off-season.

"We wouldn't likely have any off-season," Schramm explained.

Landry viewed Meredith as a sinner and a rebel. Landry told his players that their priorities should be God, family and football, in that order.

Meredith told *Playboy* that their biggest disagreements involved play calling. Sometimes Landry would send in a play, and Meredith wouldn't pay attention. Meredith liked to sing and tell jokes in his huddles. He'd say, "OK, just run the last play again."

Landry did a slow burn.

He spoke disparagingly about his QB to the team, the press and the fans. That was supposed to motivate Meredith. It did not.

Linebacker Lee Roy Jordan says in *The Last Cowboy* that he was very close to Meredith and that Landry didn't know how sensitive his quarterback was. "He really hurt Don's feelings. After a while, it was like he dreaded going out there."

Jordan said Landry didn't know how to handle players who had problems outside of football. "Married life, divorces, and so forth. He didn't know how to relate to that, and Don always had a lot of personal stuff going on."

Blackie Sherrod coined a moniker: "Mount Landry." Sherrod explained, "He was unflappable.... He was there in his unflinching granite form, yesterday, today and tomorrow."

Once he was asked which was tougher, coaching pro football or belly-flopping a bomber. "It's about the same," he said. "If you lose your cool in either situation, it's a disaster."

Tom Landry was inducted into the Pro Football Hall of Fame in 1990.

CHAPTER 26

OWNER CLINT MURCHISON JR.

WERE IT NOT for Clint Murchison Jr. there likely would be no Dallas Cowboys. All odds were against him, and still he pulled it off.

He was a genius, a graduate of the Massachusetts Institute of Technology, but with limited social skills. He couldn't make small talk, and his meetings rarely lasted beyond a couple of minutes.

He was known for his trademark burr haircut, thick horn-rimmed glasses and, always, white short-sleeved shirts, no matter the weather. Like Tom Landry, Murchison could pass you in the hallway and not acknowledge your presence. Their minds were elsewhere.

Clint was the son of one of the world's richest men, Clint Sr., who was the ultimate Texas oilman wheeler dealer. Senior described his financial empire as "financing by finagling." He got his start by trading one oil lease for money to buy a second. Always being in deep debt was just part of the plan.

Senior's advice to his sons had a lyrical ring to it: "Money is like manure. If you spread it around, it does a lot of good. But if you pile it up in one place, it stinks like hell."

Like his dad, Junior tried to do everything big. As big as Texas. He built a 43,000-square-foot home, and that's large even by Dallas standards.

Jane Wolfe, author of *The Murchisons*, learned that Junior and his brother, John, owned well over 100 companies. They dabbled in real estate, construction, insurance, banks, hotels, country clubs, TV stations, pipe-lines, oil and gas, an air-line, a candy company, an amusement park and a New York book pub-lisher.

Junior had a straight-forward philosophy. "If you are going to owe money, owe more than you can pay. Then the lenders can't afford to foreclose."

When Senior learned that Junior intended to build Texas Stadium, he said, "That's going to break that boy."

Unfortunately, history has mostly forgotten the oversized role Cowboys founder and original owner Clint Murchison Jr., a genius, played in bringing the NFL to North Texas.

But it wasn't the stadium. It was a mountain of debt, piled like manure. Simply, he owed more than he could pay.

CHAPTER 27

I CAN SIGN TEX'S NAME

IN JANUARY 1966, the Cowboys played the Baltimore Colts in what was dubbed the Losers Bowl. They were the third-place teams in the NFC and the AFC, and each had lost a playoff game trying to reach the Super Bowl.

Eisenberg writes that the Cowboys weren't allowed to bring their wives or girlfriends, and that the Colts had better accommodations. At a dog racing track, a special section was roped off for the Colts but not for the Cowboys.

Meredith was offended by his team executives' treatment of their players. He announced in the hotel bar that everybody could drink for free.

"Don't worry," he assured everyone. "I can sign Tex's name."

"We all just helped ourselves," Bob Lilly told Eisenberg.

Lilly recalled, "Well, after about a month we got these letters from Tex saying we owed him $200 apiece. I don't think he ever collected, but he was very angry."

CHAPTER 28

THE CIGAR STORY

"I SHOULDN'T be telling you this, but it's too funny to keep," backup QB Jerry Rhome told writer Steve Perkins. "You know how Don all the time is smoking those cigars? We're in the quarterback meeting and Tom is drawing a whole bunch of plays on the board. Don starts fooling around with his cigar, twirling it in his fingers, making like a symphony conductor. He's got it spinning pretty good when Tom turns around and sees him, and Don sticks the lighted end in his mouth.

"I mean, he spit tobacco and ashes and cigar and everything all over the room. Me and Craig [Morton] nearly fell out. Tom didn't crack a smile. He just looked at him. He said, 'You getting all this, Don?' And Don said, 'Yes, sir.'"

CHAPTER 29

POISON PEN CARTWRIGHT

GRANTLAND RICE wrote the most famous opening paragraph in American sports journalism. In 1924, he nicknamed the legendary backfield of the Notre Dame Fighting Irish football team "the Four Horsemen of Notre Dame."

It went like this: "Outlined against a blue-gray October sky the Four Horsemen rode again. In dramatic lore they are known as famine, pestilence, destruction and death. These are only aliases. Their real names are: Stuhldreher, Miller, Crowley and Layden."

When the Cowboys played the Browns at the Cotton Bowl in 1965 in front of a then record crowd (76,251), they were only one yard away from tying the game. On first and goal at the Browns' 1-yard line with four chances for a touchdown, Meredith threw the ball instead of running it. The pass was tipped and intercepted. *One yard away!* The booing was fierce. It grew even louder after Meredith threw a second interception. The Cowboys lost 24-17.

The next day's *Dallas Morning News* carried a Gary Cartwright story with this lead paragraph: "Outlined against the gray sky rode the Four Horsemen: Pestilence, Fame, Death and Meredith."

Maybe Cartwright didn't know the inspiration for that line came from the Book of Revelation in the New Testament. The four horsemen of the apocalypse were conquest, war, famine and death. But Cartwright would face his own journalistic apocalypse.

Meredith was trying to get the ball to receiver Frank Clarke. But Meredith didn't call the play. Landry did.

Buddy Dial said the real problem was Landry didn't create any goal-line run plays for that game, only passing plays. But Landry never said that, and Meredith took all the blame.

Dial said, "Don and I talked about it. He hated 'Poison Pen' Cartwright. He hated him! Gary was a wormy little old devil. Cartwright was so negative about everybody, and he really had it in for Meredith."

Pete Gent recalled that the players held a private team meeting without coaches about Cartwright. "They all wanted to kill him, and Meredith kept saying, 'You can't. It's his job. He's just doing his job like we're doing ours.' All the offensive linemen were particularly furious because they have a real pride about protecting their quarterback."

Cartwright's story, arguably a hit piece, hurt Meredith's confidence. He was failing on the field because of his benching. He feared for his job because Landry had drafted two quarterbacks who were waiting in the wings — Craig Morton and Jerry Rhome. And his marriage had flopped, so he was in trouble off the field, too.

Dial: "He wanted to be successful in both places. He really loved his family. He wanted to be a good father, a good husband, a good guy. And he wanted to win so bad. He wasn't a loser. What he went through would have killed an ordinary man."

It was one of the low moments of Meredith's professional life.

Cartwright said later, "In a column I said Meredith was a loser. That was stupid. Meredith wasn't a loser. I was."

Meredith may have despised Cartwright, but he didn't feel that way about all sports journalists.

Bill Mercer, now 98, the longtime Cowboys play-by-play announcer on KLIF/570 AM, has his own favorite story: One day in the locker room he was doing a pregame interview with a player. Landry came storming through and demanded, "What are you doing in here, Bill?" He told Mercer to go up to the broadcast booth.

Meredith was getting dressed, noticed, and yelled over, "Hey, Bill. What's going on with Landry?"

Mercer told him, and Meredith said, "Aw, well, he yells sometimes but not very often."

Perhaps because of that, Meredith summoned Mercer over and said, "I'm going to make you a hero."

"Oh really?"

Meredith explained how every Cowboys game began with a handoff to Don Perkins. But not this time. Meredith told Mercer to alert his broadcast audience to the unexpected.

"You better say that because I'm changing up the play," Meredith said.

On the air, Mercer played along. He told his listeners, "I have a feeling this is going to be different today."

On the first play, Meredith handed the ball off to a different player. "I guess I was right," Mercer bragged into the mic.

Later Mercer confessed on air. "I finally said, 'OK, guys, he told me ahead of time that he was going to do it, that he was going to make me a hero.'

"That was Don Meredith. I loved Don Meredith."

CHAPTER 30

COOL

IF THERE'S one word to associate with Meredith's life, it most certainly is not "loser."

The word is *cool.*

"This is about the coolest guy walking the planet," retired WFAA-TV sports anchor Dale Hansen said.

"He was a confident quarterback," defensive lineman Cole said. "He had such charisma. He had one of those memorable voices. When he entered a room, he lit up the room."

One time the Cowboys' plane was preparing for takeoff and Meredith was sitting with wide receiver Pete Gent. "They gave us two beers, and we would smuggle whiskey in," Gent said in an oral history.

"Don says, 'I'm going to drink my first beer before we take off. I'll save the second one for later.'

"We started down the runway, and we heard this tremendous bang. Everyone just sat straight up in their seats. The plane shut down, and we skidded to the edge of the runway. I could hear guys whimpering in the back of the plane.

"The pilot came on and said, 'We think we just had a little snow that blew through the engine. We're going to try it again.'"

Ice had broken off the wing and been sucked into the engine. Some players were freaking out. Meredith announced to Gent, "I think I'll have my second beer now. I don't want to waste it."

Two hours passed. The plane was de-iced repeatedly. When it lifted off, Garrison recalled, even the flight attendants were worried.

Bob Lilly announced that the end was near. "We've all had it, baby. It's all over! We're in trouble!"

Gent shouted, "Joe Don! We're gonna crash!"

A rookie asked Meredith, who was drinking his beer and smoking a cigarette, if he was scared.

Meredith took a long drag, smiled and said, "Naw, it's been a good run, ain't it?"

CHAPTER 31

MVP

In 1966, the big fashion is Nehru jacket. The song: "California Dreaming" by the Mamas and the Papas. The book: Truman Capote's *In Cold Blood*. The TV show: "Batman." The Vietnam War: The number of U.S. troops killed tripled from the year before. The NFL-AFL: Negotiations for a merger were finalized.

Sports: Don Meredith finally had an offensive line that protected him and gave him time to throw. What a difference. He was mostly healthy and exceptionally productive.

After routinely losing their first six seasons, 1966 was the Cowboys' year with budding superstars Mel Renfro, Bob Lilly and Lee Roy Jordan commanding respect. "In '66, it exploded," sportswriter Frank Luksa said.

Curt Sampson wrote in *D Magazine*, "With time to throw, you could see the basketball magician in the quarterback, the ball handler with unusual touch and flair."

In the home opener, the Cowboys beat the Giants 52-7. Next, they beat the Minnesota Vikings 28-17. The streak continued with a 47-14 win over the Atlanta Falcons. Then they pounded the Philadelphia Eagles 56-17.

Meredith puts it all together for the 1966 season, his best.
He dominates and wins Most Valuable Player.

In their first four games, the Meredith-led Cowboys scored an astounding 183 points. They came down to earth their next game—a tie with the St. Louis Cardinals.

They finished the season with their first winning record—10-3-1—and won the Eastern Division. No expansion team had done so well, so quickly.

Meredith called most of the plays that year. His friend Pete Gent, the wide receiver, told Eisenberg, "His refusal to let Landry control the team was the key to that first winning season. Everything changed."

Walt Garrison recalled, "He could pick a defense apart. He'd call a play in the huddle, and you'd think it was the stupidest play ever, and it was the smartest because he'd set defenses up. He'd say, 'Hey guys, we're going to run this, and it's not going to work now, but we're setting it up to use later in the game, and it'll work then.' He was on another level from the rest of us as far as that kind of stuff."

In his outstanding 1966 season Meredith rushed for 242 yards and five touchdowns. He passed for 2,805 yards and 24 touchdowns. His passing yardage was the most of his career. He threw only 12 interceptions, averaging fewer than one per game.

He won the Bert Bell Award, a most valuable player honor presented by the Maxwell Football Club. Voters included team owners, coaches and national and local media. Landry was named Coach of the Year, too.

1966 also was the first time the Cowboys played a home game on Thanksgiving Day. That tradition contributed mightily to increasing the team's exposure.

But 1966 is mostly remembered as the breakthrough season, the one that set the standard for all of the winning seasons and playoff games to come later.

The Cowboys played in their first meaningful playoff game New Year's Day 1967, against Landry's nemesis, the Packers. The winner would advance to the first "AFL-NFL World Championship Game." You might know that event by a new name.

The Super Bowl.

CHAPTER 32

LEADERSHIP THROUGH LAUGHTER

OFFENSIVE TACKLE Jim Boeke explained Meredith's leadership qualities, and it sounds quite similar to Joe Don from Mount Vernon High.

"If Meredith had led us over a cliff, I would have been the first one to follow," Boeke told Eisenberg. "He was that great a leader. All the guys liked him and wanted to play for him. He didn't just hang out with the receivers and running backs. He hung out with the linemen. He made everyone feel important. He just had an incredible way of motivating people."

He motivated the best way he knew—through humor.

"He was a quarterback on and off the field. He ran the show, and everybody followed," Garrison wrote. "And if there wasn't a show going, he'd make one. He'd get up and sing, tell old stories, dance.

"He was a natural born celebrity. Whether he walked into a beer joint or a black-tie affair, Joe Don was the center of attention. And if he wasn't when he got there, he would be

within a couple min-
utes. That's just the
way it was. Don didn't
plan it that way. That
was his style."

Garrison told the
story of how in 1966
Meredith bestowed
on him a nickname he
hated—Puddin. It was
the last away game
and Meredith realized
it was his final chance
to partake in the tradi-
tion of getting a rookie
slap-happy drunk the
night before a game.

Don Meredith's card for the 1968 season.

Garrison longed for a nickname like Flash or Great Hands, but no way. Not with Meredith in charge.

The night before the Steelers game, Meredith called Garrison on the hotel phone.

"Walt, what are you doing for supper tonight?"

"Oh, I think I'll get some room service, watch a little TV and get to bed early."

"No, you're not," Meredith said. "Be down in the lobby in 30 minutes."

Garrison explained, "Now a rookie in those days did not question a veteran, especially not Meredith."

When he arrived in the lobby, Meredith was waiting for him in a chauffeur's cap. He had a limousine outside. He was the driver. Buddy Dial, Dan Reeves and Lee Roy Jordan were with them.

"What do you want to drink tonight?" Meredith asked.

"Oh, iced tea or something," Garrison answered.

"No, I mean what do you want to *drink*?"

"Bourbon and seven?"

"OK, you drink a drink every time I drink, and I'm paying for it."

At the restaurant, Meredith told the waiter, "Bring him a Crown Royal Mist."

Garrison knew that with crushed ice and bourbon there's no bite, so you can drink more.

After two or three, he slowed down. Meredith was drinking Scotch like it was lemonade.

Garrison poured his drink into a nearby potted plant. Meredith caught him. He scowled and said, "Don't ever do that again!" Garrison drank more that night than ever.

The next morning, he could barely make it to breakfast. Meredith looked like he had slept for 48 hours. "He's bouncing around. He's singing and humming. He's laughing and telling jokes, and I'm just barely managing to keep my eggs down."

Near the end of the game, the Cowboys were winning big. Meredith asked Landry to put Garrison in as a running back. "Hey, you!" Landry called out to Garrison, who always thought Landry didn't know his name.

In the huddle, Meredith asked, "Hey, Walt, how's it going?"

Garrison was so hung over that his head felt like a Chinese gong.

"I've been reading all your clippings," Meredith said. "You were a hotshot in college. Let's see what you got."

Meredith called a play where Garrison takes the ball and runs up the middle. Garrison gained a yard.

"That ain't gonna do it," Meredith said back in the huddle. "You were All-American. Let's try that again."

He called the same play, and this time Garrison got nine yards and a first down.

"Now that's better. Let's run it again."

Garrison threw up in the huddle and then two Steelers crushed him on the next play. Back in the huddle Meredith scolded him and called him a female body part, a word he said he knew he couldn't use so he changed it to Puddin, or sometimes Little Puddin.

Sadly for Garrison, the name stuck. But Puddin earned respect by getting out there. His teammates considered him tough. Meredith took Puddin under his wing and could pick on the rookie, but he wouldn't let anybody else do it.

CHAPTER 33

ROOKIE ROAST

PUDDIN PERFORMED a trick that Meredith loved. He'd walk into a bar with his mouth full of lighter fluid and strike a match. Flames would shoot out six feet.

Meredith would wake Puddin up for "the rookie roast." They'd go downstairs to the dorm where the rookies were sleeping after a hard day of practice. They'd open a door and Meredith would whisper, "OK, do it, do it!" As the ball of fire shot across the room, the rookies would wake up terrified.

"That's good, Walt. Next room."

"Got to be a ritual," Puddin said.

CHAPTER 34

PREGAME SHOCKER

THE COWBOYS were preparing for their biggest game ever. The winner of the New Year's Day 1967 Cowboys-Packers playoff would play the top AFC team in the first championship game eventually labeled the Super Bowl. The Packers were the NFL's best. The Cowboys were only in their sixth year.

The night before at a team meeting someone whispered to Garrison, "You see what happened to Meredith?"

Word spread that he had fallen through a plate-glass window while out shopping. He wouldn't be able to play, and he needed 24 stitches to sew up his face.

"Meredith comes in and is completely dejected," Garrison wrote. "His head is hung down real low. And there was this big bloody scar across his face. It was gruesome. My heart just stopped when I saw him because the chances of winning suddenly weren't any good anymore."

When Coach Landry finished talking, Meredith stood and peeled the bloody scar off his face. He had hired a Hollywood makeup man.

"The whole place just exploded with laughter," Garrison wrote. "Sigmund Freud couldn't have done a better job of relaxing us. Here we were, a young expansion team, first time in the playoffs, and we were going to face Lombardi's Packers. And Meredith just turned it into a big joke. And the next day we went out and played a heck of a ball game."

DESPERATION PASS

THE FINAL MINUTES of that Jan. 1, 1967 game were excruciating. The Cowboys were a yard or so away from scoring and tying it up. An offsides penalty pushed the ball back to the 6-yard line.

Dan Reeves got poked in the eye during a play and had double vision. Later, he regretted not pulling himself out of the game.

Meredith threw to him, but he dropped the ball.

The 1966 season came down to one play. It was fourth down at the 6-yard line. For a reason never explained, Bob Hayes was out there playing tight end. But he should not have been on a goal-line play, and he didn't know he was supposed to block and protect the quarterback.

A Packers lineman easily bypassed Hayes, grabbed Meredith by the jersey and slung him around. Meredith avoided the sack and sidearmed a desperation pass into the end zone, praying that someone could catch it.

Someone did.

The ball was intercepted.

The Packers won 34-27, their second consecutive NFL championship and fourth in six years. The headline in

The Dallas Morning News: "Cowboy Season Falls One Yard Short."

Murchison cracked wise, "Well, I guess we don't want to give the fans too much, too soon, do we?"

The Packers played Kansas City (formerly the Texans) in the first NFL-AFL championship game, with the Packers winning 35-10. Imagine if the two archrivals from Dallas had played each other instead.

There would be a Cowboys-Packers rematch soon enough. Some call it one of the greatest games in NFL history.

Sportswriter Sam Blair wrote that even though Green Bay had won, it felt like in defeat, Dallas may have launched a new dynasty. "As darkness closed in on the Cotton Bowl on January 1, 1967, the Packers hurried away to begin preparations for the first Super Bowl. But the Cowboys had emerged as the team of the future."

CHAPTER 36

ICE BOWL

ONE YEAR LATER, after the Cowboys' 9-5 record in 1967, they beat the Browns in a playoff game 52-14. The big play was an 86-yard Meredith pass to Hayes.

When Landry took Meredith out at the start of the fourth quarter to save him for the big game, Meredith shook hands with each of the offensive players in the huddle. He slowly trotted off the field to a boisterous ovation.

The win set up a rematch for the right to play in Super Bowl II. This second Cowboys-Packers playoff game is recognized as a classic. Many books were written about it. Titles include:

Football's Most Unforgettable Game
The Game That Changed the NFL
The Game that Will Never Die

Saturday before the game, the players practiced on Lambeau Field in 15 degree weather. Coach Lombardi invited reporters to see his "electric blanket" to protect the field from freezing. He showed them how coils had been laid in a grid the length of the field, six inches below the surface and a foot apart. Then he showed them the small control room below the stands.

"All these lights are blinking, and he's like a mad scientist in there," one writer recalled.

Game day. Players couldn't believe their hotel wakeup call: "Good morning. It's sunny and 17 degrees below zero."

At the stadium, signs announced, "THIS FIELD IS ELEC-TRIFIED." Only it wasn't.

"The field was exactly like playing on an ice rink," Garrison wrote. "It was one big solid piece of ice."

Author David Maraniss wrote in his Lombardi biography, *When Pride Still Mattered*, that every breath "felt like an arrow shooting into their lungs."

Two days before the legendary Ice Bowl game against the Packers in horrible conditions, Meredith relaxes in his hotel room answering questions from reporters.

A cup of coffee froze before you could drink it. Frank Gifford told the TV audience, "I think I'll take another bite out of my coffee."

When someone told Lombardi the field was frozen, he said that couldn't happen. "What the heck are you talking about?" he demanded.

Lombardi had spent $80,000 on his giant, buried electric blanket, but it being underground and covered with a tarp overnight trapped the heat and created condensation. When the tarp was removed, the moist turf immediately froze.

The window on the press box was completely fogged. Someone bought cans of window deicer.

Landry had icicles sticking out of his nostrils. So did almost everyone else, and they were told not to remove them because that could damage the membranes. Refs, players and coaches were told to smear Vaseline on their lips, nose and mouth.

The Cowboys equipment manager went to every store he could find to buy rolls of Saran Wrap so the players could keep their feet warm.

The game never should have been played that day. While the Cowboys came out for warm-ups wearing every possible layer of clothing, the Packers, in a psych-out, wore T-shirts. Unlike the Cowboys, the 50,000 Lambeau Field fans knew how to dress—many layers with ski masks covering their faces, and pint bottles in all available pockets.

At kickoff, the field temperature was 13 below zero, wind chill minus 46. The football felt "like a frozen pumpkin," one writer shared. Meredith had a hard time getting a grip. Mike Shropshire, who wrote *The Ice Bowl*, said the Cowboys didn't know if they were playing for the NFL crown or the Stanley Cup.

It was so cold that when the referee blew his metal whistle on the opening play and then pulled it out of his mouth it peeled the skin off his lip. A timeout was called while someone went in search of plastic whistles. The officials decided to use verbal commands instead.

Players could hear the crunch of ice under their feet. Ice chips caused by cleats were like slivers of broken glass that cut uniforms and skin when a player hit the ground.

Early in the game, Dan Reeves got hit in the face and his teeth cut through his lip, but he didn't bleed. Only when he stood near a space heater did the blood start gushing.

As the sun dropped behind the stadium, shadowy conditions grew worse. Several Packers changed into tennis shoes for better traction. The Cowboys had been told field conditions would be fine and didn't pack extra shoes.

Meredith was so cold that his mouth froze, and he had trouble calling plays in the huddle.

Players could only run straight ahead. If they tried to make a cut, they'd slip and fall. Meredith had a difficult time throwing under those conditions.

Near the end, Dallas had the ball and halfback Reeves faked a sweep. He threw a 50-yard touchdown pass to Lance Rentzel, and the Cowboys led 17-14.

In a final 68-yard drive, Packers quarterback Bart Starr brilliantly led his team to within 12 inches of the end zone.

Like the year before, the game came down to a yard, but this time the Packers had the first and goal. They could have kicked a field goal to tie and go into sudden death overtime.

Lombardi said later he wanted the game to end so the fans could get out of the cold.

Nobody expected a quarterback sneak. Not on this field with such high stakes. But that's what happened. Starr kept the ball and pushed it over the goal line. It is still called one of the most dramatic touchdowns in league history.

Packers won 21-17. So close. Again.

Back in the locker room some players had frostbite. The players were told to take cold showers because hot water could have peeled off their skin. Didn't matter. The showers ran out of hot water.

The Packers later revealed an advantage. They noticed that when an upcoming play didn't involve Hayes, he tucked his hands down his pants to keep warm. That removed the Cowboys' No. 1 playmaker. What an advantage!

In his autobiography, Hayes, a Floridian, said the extreme cold confused him. He accidentally went on the field with the kick blocking team, of which he was not a member. He also ran toward the Packers' huddle, instead of his own.

"I was so cold I literally could not think any longer," he wrote.

When they returned to Dallas, Murchison called Hayes in and told him not to worry about the critics, and he offered this advice:

"Next time try not to put your hands in your pants."

CHAPTER 37

A STAR IS BORN

ON THE POSTGAME show Frank Gifford, the former Giants standout turned CBS broadcaster, asked the producers if he could visit the dejected Cowboys. "Why don't we get a camera in here and interview some of the losers here, too? They only lost by a quarterback sneak. And we've got plenty of time to fill."

The producer answered, "Frank, they won't do that. You can't get any of those guys to come on, and we can't ask them. It just isn't done, man."

"So let's be the first," Gifford said. "I think I can get Meredith to talk with me."

"If you feel that strongly, go ahead and take a shot."

Gifford asked. "Don, why don't you come on and say what you feel about today? It's not like you guys got killed. You got beat on a frozen home field by a lousy quarterback sneak."

"You really think I should?"

"Yeah, I really do."

Meredith said yes.

A camera and lights were brought over from the winners' locker room. Meredith's No. 17 jersey was covered with blood. He had a black eye and a huge bruise below his eye.

Live on national TV, Gifford asked, "Don, you came so close. How does it feel to lose this one?"

"The way I look at it is we didn't really lose it. Dadgummit, we didn't lose anything."

As Gifford wrote in his autobiography, *The Whole 10 Yards*, "Don proceeded to do something highly un-Don-like. He poured his heart out in public. With his voice choking on emotions, he talked about how proud he was of the guys he played with, how hard they had played that day, how awful he felt for them, how he blamed himself for the loss, but how losing like that was really like winning even though it almost felt like dying."

"I feel like I died," Meredith added. "I can't describe how cold it was. All I can say is it hurt just to breathe."

Gifford's take: "It was a passionate, spontaneous, no B.S. television moment. It was wonderful."

Afterwards, Meredith received hundreds of sympathy cards from TV viewers who felt his pain.

The next morning Gifford called Meredith to thank him.

Meredith told him, "By God, ol' buddy, you won't believe what's been goin' on! I'm getting calls from all these people in your business. They want me to go on talk shows. They want me to go on quiz shows. They even want me for a TV movie."

Gifford sensed instantly what had happened. "The people who create celebrities in America caught a glimpse of the deeply feeling man behind the devil-may-care image—and they loved what they saw. Television-wise, you might say those few minutes of airtime put Don Meredith in play."

He was in play all right. Among those who watched and was impressed was ABC Sports boss Roone Arledge.

Play-by-play man Bill Mercer sat behind Meredith on the way home. "He was in tears," he recalled. "Meredith said, 'We would have won if I played better.'"

CHAPTER 38

ICE BOWL BLUES

MEREDITH was miserable. His wife, Cheryl, told *Sport* magazine: "Don may get aggravated during the season, but he gets over it quickly. Except that one time. After that Green Bay game he was down for a month. He just couldn't snap out of it. He was depressed."

Tex Schramm would say the loss accelerated the myth of America's Team, launched after the previous Green Bay smackdown. The second big defeat showed that the Cowboys had more grit than they knew.

Meredith told *Playboy* that if the game had been played "in the rain, in a windstorm, in a desert, anywhere we could've gotten some footing" the Cowboys would have won. They couldn't do their normal plays on the frozen field.

"In the first half," he told Blackie Sherrod, "I was very conscious of the cold. In the calls I made, I tried to take into consideration a lot of factors. Is the field too slick for this particular play? Should I stay with the simple stuff? On a pass, I'd think, well, I have to lay it out there soft because the receivers' hands are so cold. I can't pop it. I was too cautious.

"At halftime, I thought, to hell with that. Then I just threw the best I could."

A week after the game, on "The Tonight Show," the guests were Meredith and Starr. Johnny Carson asked if the Packers would have had time for another play.

"You wouldn't have," Meredith interrupted. "You sure wouldn't have."

He said, "I can't describe how cold it was…. The field was so bad. We thought we had an advantage in our speed, our quickness, our multiple formations. We had studied hard and knew what to do. Suddenly we couldn't do anything we had done all season."

Landry said of the winning quarterback sneak, "It was a dumb call, but now it's a great play." He added that you could tell the real Cowboys. "They're the ones with the frozen fingers and broken hearts."

The game soon had a new name. Forevermore it would be the Ice Bowl, where the Cowboys had to battle three opponents—the Packers, the record-setting cold and the hard-as-concrete field.

Vince Lombardi's name is on the Super Bowl trophy. But what if both Cowboys-Packers games had gone the other way? Would it be called the Tom Landry trophy?

Instead of Lombardi carried off the field on his players' shoulders, would it have been Landry? We'll never know. But as sports columnist Jim Reeves said, "Hell had indeed frozen over."

CHAPTER 39

LOMBARDI'S FOLLY

Dᴵᴰ Vɪɴᴄᴇ Lᴏᴍʙᴀʀᴅɪ cheat to win that game? It's a sensitive subject.

General Electric, which designed and built the underground heating system, guaranteed it would create "September-like" conditions. Instead of a frozen field, players would experience soft, frost-free turf.

Lombardi learned the engineer had shut his gizmo down because it was doing more harm than good. He knew he would get blamed and feared it would be called "Lombardi's Folly." His son, Vince Jr., said his dad would be accused of tampering with the heating system to make the field worse for Dallas. Opinions varied.

Schramm said, "Vince, as everybody knows, was a person of genuine character, and he had real strong feelings about taking unfair advantage of a situation."

Chuck Carlson, author of *Ice Bowl '67*, wrote that rumors swirled for years that Lombardi intentionally turned off the system to slow down the Cowboys. But observers at the time said that Lombardi's angry reaction to the faulty electrical system shutdown proved there was no way he planned this.

After all, what slowed down the Cowboys also slowed down the Packers.

But what if Lombardi did supervise the heating failure?

His pregame TV program—"The Vince Lombardi Show"—offered several clues about his state of mind, as seen from part of the transcript of Michael Meredith's terrific documentary, *First Cowboys*.

"Dallas is the big game of the year," Lombardi said on TV. "We're real happy we're going to play in Green Bay. Let me say that."

He bragged about the heating system. "Our field is going to be in good shape—unless something happens to that electric blanket we have out there.

"I'm thinking sometime maybe I ought to go out and pull the switch and cut down on the..."

"The power bill?" the cohost blurted.

"No, no," Lombardi said. "To cut down on that speed that the Dallas team has."

I showed the video to Traci Brown, a deception detection expert. She watched the coach's body language and listened to his words.

When she was done, she announced, "He planned on doing that."

How could she tell?

"You don't start talking about what happens when it doesn't work. He's nervous. See how he starts fidgeting and moving forward [in his seat] and all of a sudden he's laughing.

"Oh, and then he rubs his hands together. When you rub your hands together in the speed that he did, that says positive expectation like excitement.

"He is so excited to turn that off. He's fully planning on turning it off. Why would you say, if you spent $80,000 on a field—which is a lot of money back then—why would you say 'unless I turn it off' or it doesn't work?"

She watched the video again and concluded, "There's no mystery here. It's completely his plan. He seems very entertained by his plan…. He's revealing his plan right here."

Did Lombardi flip a switch? The ice rink certainly took key scorer Bob Hayes out of the game by, as Lombardi said, "cutting down on that speed that the Dallas team has."

Lilly said in Pettis Norman's biography that the Cowboys honestly thought it froze. "I don't think Lombardi would tinker with the underground heating unit. I think the weather did it. Green Bay's favorite play was the outside running play, the Power Sweep, and they tried some outside running plays. They slipped down, too."

Lee Roy Jordan said in the Norman biography, "We'll never know what happened to the electric grid installed beneath Lambeau Field to prevent the field from freezing. I wouldn't be surprised if Lombardi did something to give his team an advantage, playing on a skating rink rather than a football field."

Cornerback Mel Renfro said of Lombardi's Folly: "We couldn't battle the Packers and the elements and the weather at the same time. They couldn't get the heating function beneath Lambeau Field to work. It mysteriously malfunctioned. In my opinion it was no mystery. Lombardi pulled the plug on that electric grid, no doubt in my mind. He knew he had to have leverage because he knew how talented we were.

"There was no way they could win unless something like that happened. We lived in Dallas, Texas, where it's 90 degrees, 100 degrees. We're used to warm weather. The cold was not our friend. Lombardi knew that and took advantage of that. I'll believe that to the day I die."

Play-by-play man Mercer said he didn't believe Lombardi would do that. "I hate to think that about a man who was a great coach and greatly admired."

CHAPTER 40

ART IMITATES LIFE

WIDE RECEIVER Pete Gent let his hair grow long (first Cowboy to do so), which disturbed his head coach. His rebelliousness played out in other ways, most famously the novel, *North Dallas Forty,* his 1973 thinly veiled exposé of shenanigans in the NFL.

Gent said the title was a reference to the forced segregation that kept Blacks out of North Dallas. Team rosters had 40 players at the time.

The book announced on page 6 that all of the characters were fictitious and that "any resemblance to actual persons, living or dead, is purely coincidental." But the world knew that quarterback Seth Maxwell, played by country music star Mac Davis in the 1979 Paramount movie, was based on Don Meredith.

The players on the North Dallas Bulls were party animals, womanizing ruffians, propped up by shots and pills, a view many real players disavowed. "The picture he painted of the NFL was completely foreign to me," Pettis Norman wrote in his autobiography.

Meredith was offered the lead role in the film but turned it down.

"The book didn't seem to bother him," Gent said. "He was glad to see it. But when it came out as a movie, his attitude changed."

Frank Gifford said Meredith was "very hurt and very angry."

When the book *North Dallas Forty* by former Cowboys player Pete Gent comes out satirizing the Cowboys, Meredith likes it. But he's not a fan of the movie. The lead character is supposedly based on him.

It was not an image Meredith wanted the world to see.

Writers tried to show that image through novels written by sportswriters. He likely is the only NFL quarterback to have three novels come out with characters based on him.

Dan Jenkins wrote *Semi-Tough* with its Meredith-like quarterback, Billy Clyde Puckett. Gary Cartwright wrote *The Hundred Yard War*, featuring Meredith-like running back Rylie Silver.

A.J. Chilson wrote a delightful children's book about Meredith, but, until now, there has never been a full-length book expressly devoted to Meredith's life.

It's one of the great Meredith mysteries: Why didn't he tell his own story?

LOVED AND HATED

IMAGINE HEARING your name over the public address system, and thousands of boos rain down. Booing continued to be a problem.

Author Eisenberg said fans believed Meredith didn't care. They thought his wisecracks and singing player routine showed a blasé attitude.

"Plus," he said, "they were losing."

Dallas Morning News columnist Bob St. John wrote that Meredith was "the most cheered, booed, loved and hated athlete ever to play in the Cotton Bowl."

Sportswriter Frank Luksa, who covered the Cowboys for 40 years, underlined that, saying Meredith "was vilified more than any other athlete in this town ever. He was booed on sight in pregame, when he was in the game, and when he came out of the game."

At first Meredith sloughed it off, joking that "they boo me because they know me so well." He said he trained himself to not hear the boos or the cheers. But as the boos grew louder, even when he was winning, he was sensitive. He finally complained on live TV.

The fans, he said, "are really something else. I'm getting tired of it. You know, the fun's about over…. What people fail to realize is, we're human beings. I've got feelings like anybody else. If people don't think I try, they're so wrong. I try harder than anybody because I'm the one that's out there. I don't understand it. I never booed anybody in my life, and I never will."

It got so bad that the Cotton Bowl announcer, at Landry's insistence, stopped introducing Dallas' offensive players. Only the defense was introduced, which spared Meredith a public shaming.

CHAPTER 42

THE FINAL GAME

FOR THE 1968 season Meredith prepared like never before. "For the first time," he told Cartwright, "I've cut out all appearances. It isn't that I'm getting uppity or big-time. I have made a whole bunch of appearances in the past. I'll make two or three for Jantzen and a couple for Dr Pepper, but I've scheduled them mostly all on Mondays. Then I'll tape my TV show on Tuesdays. That will give me the rest of the week to concentrate on the game. I think it will help me, especially on some of the teams we play. I'm setting up a projection deal at home so I can study films. The few times I've done it in the past, it seems I've played better. I don't know why I haven't done it more often."

That year Meredith was a *Sports Illustrated* coverboy with the headline "Dallas on top."

It was a good prediction. The team was 12-2 and led the league in scoring. Despite his many injuries, Meredith completed a career-high 55% of his passes. He threw for 2,500 yards and 21 touchdowns. The defense was first in the league.

But to make the Super Bowl, the Cowboys had to win a playoff game against the Cleveland Browns. Flush with

Meredith is popular enough that he sometimes appears on the cover
of the best-known national sports magazines.

overconfidence, team executives printed *and sold* tickets not
only for the Browns' game but for the playoff game after that.

By the third quarter of this crucial game, Meredith had
thrown three interceptions, with one of them hitting the
hands of receiver Lance Rentzel, who couldn't hold it. In a
public humiliation, with the score 24-10, Landry pulled Meredith, then 3-9 in passing, and benched him. In his place,
Craig Morton stepped in.

"I did this to have an effect on the team," Landry said.

Gent later said Landry panicked. "It cost us the game. The
idea of replacing your quarterback to have an effect on the
team is just nuts. Who pulls your starting quarterback in the

third period of a playoff game when you're only one or two touchdowns behind? Particularly when you're a team that's as explosive as we were? He [Landry] had quit. He was planning for next season. Game over."

Gent added, "The thing about criticizing Landry is how can you attack God, Mom and apple pie? The guy was a war hero."

Meredith sat on the bench in despair.

With the game all but over, Schramm walked down to the sidelines and headed for Meredith. "When he found him, he buried his head in Meredith's chest and wept," Eisenberg wrote. "Meredith wrapped his arms around Schramm. The two men hugged."

Schramm told Eisenberg, "I remember the moment very well. I was standing by the bench and he came off the field. We had tried so hard and come so far, and to see him come out of the game like that, for some reason, it just struck me as enormously sad. I don't think I thought it would be his last game. I just knew how badly he felt about not being able to do it that day. It just struck me, and I broke up. I still break up when I think about it. There was something very, very sad about it."

Morton struggled, completing only 9 of 23 passes. The Cowboys lost 31-20.

At the Cleveland airport, Meredith boarded the team flight, ate a hamburger and said to Gent, "Let's get out of here." They exited the plane, found a flight to New York and stayed with Frank Gifford for three days.

The Cowboys next played in that year's pointless Playoff Bowl. They beat the Vikings 17-13. Meredith was named game MVP.

Then it was over. His career ended on a metal bench, head lowered to his knees at Cleveland Municipal Stadium.

He thought about staying. It was hard to walk away from a $100,000-a-year job (top salary on the team). But he had his reasons to quit.

CHAPTER 43

THE MEANING OF LIFE

MEREDITH WENT to Landry's house to give him the news that he was stepping away from football. "You know, Coach," he said, "I think it's time for me to retire."

Landry didn't try to talk him out of it. He said, "Don, that's the very best thing you can do. If that's the way you feel, it's probably the right decision. I understand completely. Let's pray."

Two days later at a press conference, wearing a suit and tie, Meredith said he was there to announce his retirement.

"I have been playing football for something like 24 years. I have no distaste for the game for it's been very, very good to me. But now I want a different type of life. I want to spend more time with my two children and with my wife."

He tried to explain what was in his heart: "I'm here for a reason. I'm 31 years old, and I'm not even sure I found that reason yet. But I'm looking for it. I think I've got something else I'm supposed to do, and I'm going to find it."

Meredith decides to retire after the 1968 season. At the press conference, Landry (left) and Schramm open with kind words about Meredith, who's sitting in the background with his second wife, Cheryl, as he waits to speak.

Meredith tells reporters that he is retiring from football. "I'm here for a reason," he says. "I'm 31 years old, and I'm not even sure I found that reason yet. But I'm looking for it. I think I've got something else I'm supposed to do, and I'm going to find it."

Meredith shakes hands with Schramm (left) and Landry. It's the official end of a relationship that lasted an unforgettable decade.

Landry asserted that he did attempt to sway Meredith. "I tried to talk him out of it. But if you lose the desire to play you really shouldn't play."

Meredith said the booing didn't make him go, but other things did. Tired of Landry. A failing marriage. A daughter born with severe birth defects. And all of his injuries, so many injuries.

"If I have any regrets it's that I won't have any active part in a championship for this team, and I'm positive a championship will come," he told reporters.

Speaking about Landry, he got classy. "I have come to love the guy.... He's the finest man I've ever known. I will miss him a great deal."

Landry said he and Meredith grew close during their nine years together. "Don was a very important part of the success of the team. It certainly is a deep personal loss in seeing him step down." As a parting gift, Landry gave Meredith a leather-bound Bible.

Meredith closed out his career with 17,000 yards passing, a 50% completion rate, 135 touchdowns and 111 interceptions. He was a three-time Pro Bowl player, the NFL equivalent of an all-star team.

But he never played in a Super Bowl.

"I think Don would rather have had a good time and really didn't discipline himself like I believed you have to do to become a top quarterback," Landry said, according to Joe Nick Patoski in his book *The Dallas Cowboys: The Outrageous History of the Biggest, Loudest, Most Hated, Best Loved Football Team in America.*

Schramm tried to talk him out of quitting. Thirty-one is the perfect age for a mature quarterback. "I'm very sorry he didn't stay around long enough to win a Super Bowl. He deserved that."

CHAPTER 44

INJURIES

MEREDITH WAS 6-foot-3 and 210 pounds, but he was NFL frail. Remember as an infant his battle with polio. His nickname at SMU, aside from "Dandy Don," was "Slim." His legs were so weak looking that he sometimes stuffed his socks with shin guards while playing to buff up his legs.

"The Lord gave me a pitiful body," he once said. "But I'll just do the best I can with it."

In his autobiography, Garrison wrote that "Meredith was one of the best athletes on the Cowboys. But from the knees down Don was a wimp. His calves were like skinny old sticks of wood."

Landry said, "If Don has a weakness it's his legs. They're not big."

Without a strong offensive line season after season, Meredith was an easy target.

His rookie year, he had separated ribs, broken bones, dislocated fingers and pulled muscles. He kept playing.

In a 1964 exhibition game he tore ligaments in his left knee when legendary linebacker Ray Nitschke tackled him. He played the season on one good leg, and was sacked 58 times.

Here's a sequence of events, all too typical. Meredith gets sacked, is treated by doctors and helped into the locker room.

Meredith gets sacked. A lot. This one is from 1967 against Washington.

Courtesy of *The Fort Worth Star-Telegram* Collection, Special Collections, The University of Texas at Arlington Libraries

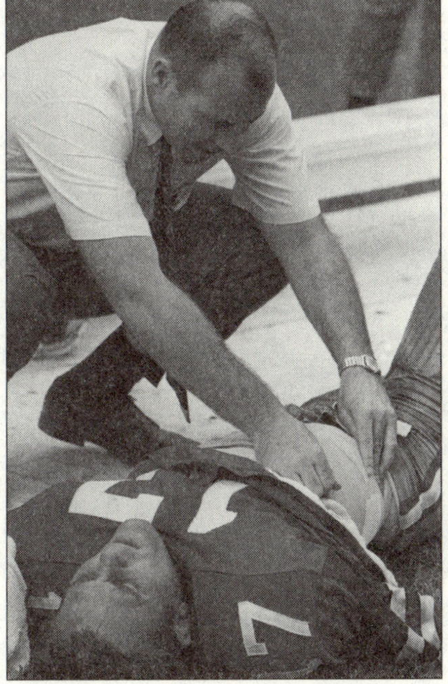

First, Meredith gets examined on the sidelines.

From the collections of the Dallas History & Archives Division, Dallas Public Library

The team doctor continues to work on Meredith. In this 1968 regular season game against the Packers, Green Bay defensive end Willie Davis grabs Meredith's helmet and breaks his nose. Meredith says his nose is broken more than a dozen times.

In this 1964 game, two of his teammates help an injured Meredith off the field. Far too often, fans watch Meredith be helped to the locker room.

For a while, offensive lineman Jim Boeke said, "it was like feeding him to the wolves back there. We were young and not blocking as well as we could. Don got hit left and right.... He got killed back there."

Dallas Times Herald writer Steve Perkins invented a new statistic: "yards lost attempting to live."

In 1967 Meredith played against Washington with a cracked rib. After the game he felt so bad the team doctor checked him into a hospital. He had pneumonia, and his lungs filled with fluid. His temperature was 105. They put him in an oxygen tent. He lost 17 pounds in a week.

Three weeks later, he was back in the lineup.

In an era before concussion protocols, he'd return to the huddle but couldn't speak because the wind was knocked out of him. Occasionally, he was sacked so hard he couldn't remember his teammates' names. Landry, asked about Meredith's grogginess, said, "Well, I can't tell the difference."

In 1968, his final year, Meredith left the hospital and went straight to a playoff game against the Browns.

One time when he was knocked out of a game, he awoke from his blackout and mumbled, "Why did I ever do it?"

"Why what?" the trainer asked.

"Why did I ever leave Mount Vernon?"

Not all injuries were from games. During the 1965 training camp, the Cowboys announced that Meredith had hurt his arm and would miss games. The rest of the story? He and Buddy Dial bought water pistols that were "like machine guns," Dial told author Golenbock. "We were having a war in the hall, and he slipped on the wet floor and hurt his arm. Of course, I got blamed for it."

"To Tom Landry," Golenbock wrote, "this injury was inexcusable because of the way it happened. There was no question, though, that Meredith had to play at a serious disadvantage." Meredith explained his ability to survive this way: "It has something to do with your masculinity. Proving your manhood. This is a very masculine game. It's hard to do that frontier stuff anymore, fording rivers and so forth, but this game sorta occupies this place for me."

In another interview, he elaborated: "I found an almost sensuous pleasure in football, in the sense that you experience it with your body. My nose was broken 14 times on various football fields, and I can't tell you that I loved getting my nose broken, but it's really something to experience that shock, to have the shock lessen and to then go beyond it. I remember feeling the warmth of the blood running out of my nose after it had been broken, and I know this sounds weird, but physically, there's pleasure in being able to extend yourself, knowing you can take yourself a step further.

"I suppose that's tied to a physical macho identification we get programmed with very early in life. We're seeing a softening of it now, but for a long time, sport was one way of defining what it means to be a man. And football, I think, represented a kind of hardcore masculinity that baseball and basketball didn't."

One time, his answer to the question about how he withstood the pain was far more simplistic. It distracted him from his divorce and losing custody of his daughter.

"In a way I welcomed those beatings after losing a wife and a daughter. It felt good."

PRANKING SAM HUFF

Sam Huff was a scary Washington linebacker who delighted in sacking Meredith. Sometimes Meredith would tease Huff that he lined up at the line of scrimmage in the wrong position. "He talked the entire game," Huff once complained. "He would be singing and talking so much over there, I don't know how he was able to concentrate."

In 1967, Meredith wore a fluid-filled flak jacket to protect his stomach and ribs. The fluid was red.

When Huff sacked him, the jacket exploded and the red liquid covered his jersey. Meredith fell and wasn't moving.

"Now you've done it, Sam," he said when he opened his eyes. "You've killed me."

Huff apologized over and over.

"It's all right, Sam. Just do me a favor. Write my mother."

When Huff figured out what was going on, he didn't laugh.

CHAPTER 46

APPLES! ORANGES! BANANAS! PEACHES!

ONE MORE football story. Long before Peyton Manning's "Omaha!" at the line of scrimmage and Dak Prescott's "Here we go!" Meredith had his own catchphrase, and at least one time, it saved him from a severe sacking.

The Steelers were whipping him good.

At the line of scrimmage Meredith shouted, "Apples! Oranges! Bananas! Peaches!" The snap was on peaches.

The Steelers laughed.

Bob Lilly wrote in his autobiography, "For the rest of the game they took it pretty easy on Don. They would just knock him down to the ground rather than trying to annihilate him. Somehow they got to see him more like a stand-up comic than the enemy."

Former Steeler Ernie Stautner, who later became the Cowboys' defensive coordinator, confirmed. "That told us he had had enough, so we quit beating on him and never did it again for the remainder of the game."

CHAPTER 47

THROW YOU A BONE

AFTER HE left football, Meredith entered the business world as a stockbroker. While trying to earn money for his clients, he lost what he had. His $100,000-a-year salary with the Cowboys dwindled to $12,000.

"I was a miserable failure," he told *Playboy*. "I just couldn't make cold calls."

He tried. "I'm working 12 hours a day. I'm up at 5:45 each morning, at the office by 7… It's different working for yourself.… I had been under the protective umbrella of the Cowboys for so long that I didn't learn to appreciate it. Now the Cowboys check doesn't come in any more. And I'm just scraping around to pay this and that off."

One potential customer convinced him this new occupation wasn't a good fit.

"The guy was a sports fan and a pretty active trader. I'd learned all these things about how you sell to a new customer. So when I called on the guy, I gave him our spiel.… Well, this guy was smoking a big ole cigar in his big ole office, and after I finished, he leaned back in his big ole chair and said, 'I'll tell you what, Don. I like you. I've always liked you. I do some investing, as you know, so every now and then I'll make it a point to throw you a bone.'

"I walked out of there thinking, 'Shoot, I can't handle that. He's gonna throw me a bone?' You expect that your name is going to get your foot in the door. Well, all it meant to me is somebody was gonna slam it on my foot."

He added, "If I had worked this hard for Tom Landry, no telling what I could have done."

Meredith also helped out his older brother, Billy Jack, who was president of Irving-based Docutel, which created the automated teller machine. Prospective customers met with Don, some Cowboys, even a few cheerleaders.

Fortunately, the TV show "The American Sportsman" invited him to go to Africa for a show hunting cape buffalo. He and Cheryl, his second wife, eagerly anticipated the adventure.

"I just wanted that trip because I was restless and uncomfortable with what I'd been doing."

When he got back, he called Frank Gifford, said he was dead broke and asked about any broadcast jobs.

No one yet knew that Dandy Don would soon find the reason he was here.

Turns out there were opportunities. Indeed there were.

CHAPTER 48

DANDY DON AND HARLEY SMYDLAPP

H IS NICKNAME was Dandy Don. Soon the entire nation would know that. Some called him simply Dandy. Merriam-Webster defines dandy as a man who gives exaggerated attention to personal appearances. A secondary meaning is being an excellent example of its kind—this milkshake is a dandy.

How did he get that nickname, and what did it mean? There are different versions of the story. In one telling, Billy Jack gave it to him.

Meredith remembered being called Dandy in college. He considered Dandy his alter ego. "To me, Dandy Don was the quarterback. That got started in college. People could write about this quarterback, but I could separate the quarterback and myself."

He had another imaginary friend. When he was 12, he saw the movie *Harvey*, in which Jimmy Stewart talks to his invisible rabbit. Meredith created his own invisible pal.

He'd talk about Harley Smydlapp as if he were real, which some found humorous and others confusing. Harley worked at Smydlapp, Smydlapp and Calhoun, "a large fact-finding organization."

"Where are they located?" the interviewer asked. "In your head?"

"Oh, no," Meredith replied. "They're everywhere, and they're retained by the American public to find out what's going on."

CHAPTER 49

ROONE

COMPILE A LIST of the most innovative people in broad-cast journalism, and Roone Arledge has to be in the top 10.

Using college football as an example, in 1960 he threw his producer hat in the ring for his network, ABC, to broadcast college football games. College football on TV was old school, a fixed camera on the 50-yard line and not much more. You could watch it as a fan would see it. Bad seats. Players so far away, they looked like little men.

Most TV sports were covered that way. Baseball Commis-sioner Ford Frick explained: "The view a fan gets at home should not be any better than that of the fan in the worst seat in the ballpark."

Arledge turned that upside down. In a weekend frenzy to make a Monday morning deadline, he wrote a planning memo for NCAA executives:

"Television has done a remarkable job of bringing the game to the viewer. Now we are going to take the viewer to the game."

"We will utilize every production technique to heighten the viewers' feeling of actually sitting in the stands and participating personally in the excitement and color.

"We must gain and hold the interest of women and others who are not fanatic followers of the sport we happen to be televising.... We will have cameras mounted on Jeeps, on mike booms, in risers or helicopters, or anything necessary to get

Roone Arledge is a television genius. Among his many achievements, he puts together the legendary "Monday Night Football" team.

the complete story of the game. We will use 'creepy-peepy' cameras to get the impact shots that we cannot get from a fixed camera—a coach's face as a man drops a pass in the clear, a pretty cheerleader just after her hero has scored a touchdown, a co-ed who brings her infant baby to the game in her arms, the referee as he called a particularly difficult play, a student hawking programs in the stands, two romantic students sharing a blanket late in a game on a cold day, the beaming face of a substitute halfback as he comes off the field after running 70 yards for a touchdown.

"The goal is to add all the excitement, wonder, jubilation and despair that make this America's number one sports spectacle." Sports have drama and stories, he wrote. "Human drama that would make the producer of a dramatic show drool. All we have to do is find it and insert it in our game coverage at the perfect moment.... In short, we are going to add show business to sports!"

NCAA officials approved, although they did ask that the fictitious shot of a co-ed and her baby get deleted from the marketing plan — for image purposes.

ABC paid a record $6 million for the rights to broadcast college football. Arledge got his chance to produce his first live sports telecast. And it was a hit! A big-time, game-changing, culture-defining hit.

CHAPTER 50

WIDE WORLD
OF SPORTS

ARLEDGE BROKE another golden rule of TV sports coverage. He begged his bosses to let him televise sporting events from around the world, games that would never make it on traditional TV: cliff diving, rodeo, curling, demolition derby, boxing, karate, skateboarding, barrel jumping, aerobatics, arm wrestling, hunting, Little League baseball, surfing and more, much more.

He called it "Wide World of Sports," and its opening stanza remains one of TV's most memorable introductions:

Spanning the globe to bring you the constant variety of sport
The thrill of victory and the agony of defeat
The human drama of athletic competition
This is ABC's Wide World of Sports.

CHAPTER 51

MONDAY NIGHT FOOTBALL

A DECADE AFTER changing college football coverage, an experienced and wiser Arledge pushed to create a new spectacle, "Monday Night Football." He had the best ally, NFL Commissioner Pete Rozelle, who had the idea in the first place.

Frank Gifford was on a plane with Arledge, and he mentioned Meredith as a candidate for the MNF booth. Arledge called Meredith and left a message. Meredith kept calling, leaving messages. Arledge didn't call back. Each time he'd leave a message Meredith grew hotter.

"Roone finally returned my call," Meredith remembered. "He gave all his reasons for not getting back to me, and I was very brash. I told him, 'Hey, I just want to see you and tell you what a horse's butt I think you are.'"

Over a meal at legendary Toots Shor's Restaurant, Arledge offered Meredith the third seat in the booth. He wrote his proposed salary on a cocktail napkin—$20,000 for one year—and handed it to Meredith, who explained that CBS had offered him the same amount, and he intended to take it.

Meredith wrote his own response on a napkin — $30,000 a year for three years.

Arledge hesitated because it was more than his budget. Meredith assured him, "It's the best $10,000 you'll ever spend."

That was a big moment. Another came when Arledge was in Japan watching a movie in Japanese that he couldn't understand and was impressed by fight scenes shown in slow motion. "What if he could do the same with football?"

In 1961, thanks to ABC engineer Bob Trachinger, ABC introduced slow-motion playbacks. It was primitive, but it worked. A slow-motion camera filmed the original live video and replayed it slower for broadcast. (In 1963 CBS producer Tony Verna unveiled a different feature called "instant replay.")

One of the greatest sports broadcasting teams of all time —
from left, Dandy Don, Howard Cosell and Frank Gifford.

When "Monday Night Football" —or MNF as it came to be known—went on the air, it was unprecedented, and the detractors howled. How could it possibly work?

Then something happened at the end of the debut Jets-Browns game. Jets QB Joe Namath threw an interception to lose the game. He stood on the field in existential agony.

Sitting in the production truck, Arledge shouted, "Look at Namath! TAKE IT!" The ABC camera showed Namath in a still-life image that depicted his immense disappointment.

"With the Namath shot," Gunther and Carter, authors of *Monday Night Mayhem*, wrote, "Arledge attained a goal that had seemed quixotic: to bring the art of still photography to the kinetic medium of television.... And in the very first edition of the most important program of his sports career, he had done it."

When Joe Namath throws an interception that cost his Jets the game on the very first "Monday Night Football" game in 1970, Arledge orders the director to focus on Namath's disappointment. That camera shot demonstrarted that the new show was something different—more artful, with a grand design of great storytelling.

The show was an immediate hit, eventually beating any competition on the other networks. As Howard Cosell would brag, "What do people talk about on Tuesday morning? They talk about me and Dandy and even Keith. We have become—if I may continue to tell it like it is—bigger than the game."

Meredith liked to say, only half joking, "We tried to not let the game get in our way."

In the print press, Cosell was getting slammed, as predicted. Meredith's reviews were glowing. Jim Murray of the *Los Angeles Times* wrote, "Meredith comes on like a riverboat gambler with a heart of gold. He seems to have the lifestyle of a guy who expected to be shot any day by a guy he dealt four aces to." Joe Fauls of the *Detroit Free Press* wrote that Meredith was the brightest thing to hit TV since somebody had the idea to invent color television.

Movie theaters and restaurants detected a sudden loss of Monday night customers. Bars had contests to determine who would have the honor of throwing a brick at a TV when Cosell came on. MNF watching parties became popular.

Even with tremendous ratings, however, everything wasn't perfect. Cosell didn't know

Howard Cosell is the most disliked sports commentator in America. But his ongoing comedy routine with Meredith corners the nation's attention on Monday nights.

it, but he was on probation for four weeks. Henry Ford II, the biggest MNF advertiser, called ABC's top brass after the first show wanting Cosell removed. Why? Too annoying. Too New York. Too Jewish.

"Get that guy off," Ford demanded. "He's hogging all the time. He talks so much I can't enjoy the football game."

Arledge responded, "Howard's doing fine. It's only been one show. The audience needs to get to know him."

After a month, Ford called back. "I want to apologize," he said. "Despite my complaints on opening night, I like the patter that's going on between Cosell and Meredith. I'm enjoying that along with the game, and I want to withdraw my objections."

CHAPTER 52

THE BANTER

COSELL AND MEREDITH jousted on live TV for hundreds of hours from 1970 to 1983.

A half dozen or so comments are ones mostly remembered.

On the 1970 debut night, Meredith showed how some boundaries of network TV would be collapsing. Talking about Cleveland receiver Fair Hooker, Meredith told the audience, "Fair Hooker. Haven't met one yet."

Once, while covering a game in Denver, Meredith said, "We're in the Mile High City, and I sure am."

He referred to then-President Richard Nixon as "Tricky Dick," the man's longtime nickname but unwise on TV where his appointees handled the renewal of government-issued broadcast licenses.

The network forced Meredith to apologize the following week.

On air, Meredith stumbled through a poor excuse for an apology.

He turned to Gifford in the booth and said, "Help me."

Gifford replied, "You got yourself into this."

Likely the best-remembered moment came during a one-sided Oakland Raiders-Houston Oilers game when director Forte asked his crew to find something interesting, a difficult assignment because most of the fans had left.

One camera operator found a guy in the end zone. Just as Forte ordered a zoom-in, the man looked straight in the camera and flashed the middle finger to America.

Cosell was uncharacteristically speechless.

Meredith chimed in: "How about that, Howard? He's telling us they're number one in the nation."

Meredith got credit for the line, but producer Dennis Lewin actually gave it to him through his earpiece.

The hits kept coming. When Cosell criticized players or coaches, Meredith liked to remind him, "Gee, Howard, nobody's perfect!"

During a Giants-Cowboys game, Cosell reminded that Gifford starred for the Giants, while Danderoo (as he sometimes called Meredith) quarterbacked the Cowboys.

"Well, gentlemen, he said, "neither of your respective teams is showing much this evening."

Meredith replied "Well, Howard, at least we do have respective teams."

Curt Sampson wrote in *D Magazine* that "Cosell would say something ponderous and self-important, the nerd's-eye view of the game delivered in as many syllables as possible," and "Dandy Don, armed with recent combat experience and bushels of East Texas charm, punctured each of Cosell's hot air balloons as they floated by. It was hilarious."

In that first year, Meredith was in the booth as the Cardinals crushed his former teammates 38-0. QB Craig Morton was Meredith's replacement.

Suddenly the crowd started chanting, "We want Meredith! We want Meredith!"

Meredith shut that down in a heartbeat. "No way you're getting me down there."

CHAPTER 53

HOWARD HATRED

MEREDITH SOMETIMES thought his life was in danger because of his association with Cosell.

"I don't like crowds to begin with, but to walk through one with Howard—man—people shout all kinds of things at him. And they're not kidding around," he told *Playboy*. "We've had bomb threats. People can be very violent toward Howard."

One threat was disturbing enough that Miami police guarded the broadcast booth.

In another incident, FBI agents stood guard in Buffalo.

Meredith said he was not surprised by the anger Cosell attracted. "When Howard burst onto the scene, he shocked our rather staid culture to the extent that he was immediately rejected."

That, plus "Howard's a New York Jew and he has all the things that set him up for bigotry and abuse."

A wary Meredith tried to avoid getting in the same limousine with Cosell. "Sometimes they shook our limos so violently they almost turned over," Gifford wrote in his autobiography.

When he used big words, often unnecessarily, it's like he's showing off, Meredith said. "And I think that's the most offensive thing about Howard."

Example: Angry that a fan interrupted the game to climb a cable near the stadium, Cosell told the TV audience, "Giffer, it is beyond my perspicacity why spectators of this once-splendiferous sport behave the way they do. How can the NFL allow this execrable rowdiness to continue?"

CHAPTER 54

BOOZE

THE MNF BOOTH was not an alcohol-free zone. Gifford didn't drink, and on occasion Danderoo would have a taste.

Cosell, on the other hand, drank at pregame parties and asked production assistants to fetch him drinks. Finally, he brought into the booth a gallon jug that he stored near his feet.

He didn't try to hide it, not even when *TV Guide* reporter Don Kowet visited for a story: "Two hours before game time Cosell is outside the ABC broadcast booth, sipping vodka from a cup."

One reason for all the drinking was the stress of office—or in this case stadium—politics. It never ended. Cosell biographer Mark Ribowsky summarized:

"Meredith said he was going to quit because Howard was making him look bad.... Then the next week, Howard was going to quit because he felt Roone was catering to Don. And Frank at various times thought those two were trying to make him look bad."

At an Eagles game Cosell was snockered before he made it to the booth. Eagles owner Leonard Tose compounded the problem by sending in two gifts — a bottle of Courvoisier and a jug of vodka martinis.

The first quarter was fine. But by the second, Cosell was stumbling over his fancy words. He couldn't say Philadelphia. In the booth, his eyes rolled back, and he fell over. In doing so, he vomited on Danderoo's new cowboy boots that he'd bought earlier that day.

"Howard's going to have to leave us now," Meredith told the TV audience. "Something's come up."

Cosell left the stadium and took a taxi to the Philadelphia airport where there were no flights home to New York. So he hired a taxi driver who warned him the fare would be high. It was $92, but Cosell arrived home at 3:45 a.m.

A few hours later when the sun came up and America was talking not about the game but about Cosell, Arledge issued a statement that Cosell had a bad reaction to medicine.

Cosell's doctor said Cosell had vertigo, an inner ear infection that causes lack of balance.

CHAPTER 55

THE HEARTLAND

TO BOLSTER his TV salary, Meredith made dozens of appearances, mostly in the South and Southwest. All people wanted to hear about was his relationship with Cosell.

"A lot of people think that Howard and I hate one another, when really, just the opposite is true," he told them. "I really love Howard. He's a beautiful guy."

Meredith told Cosell the most popular question was "How do you live with that guy, Cosell?"

"They really think we're enemies," Meredith said. "It's amazing. They keep asking me, 'What kind of guy is Cosell? What is he really like?'"

"Well," Cosell said, "what do you finally tell them?"

Meredith shrugged. "I wind up telling them you're a son of a bitch because they won't believe the truth."

CHAPTER 56

TURN OUT THE LIGHTS

MEREDITH BROUGHT phrases to the English language. He called MNF Mother Love's Traveling Freak Show. There's Dandy and Danderoo and Harley Smydlapp.

He brought one old-time phrase, denoting foolish excuse-making, back into popular usage: "If ifs and buts were candy and nuts, we'd all have a Merry Christmas."

And best known, when a lopsided win was unfolding, Meredith would sing in the booth a tune that meant America could call it a night, turn off the TV and get some sleep because the outcome was known. As Willie Nelson wrote it:

Turn out the lights. The party's over.
They say that all good things must end.
Call it a night, the party's over
And tomorrow starts the same old thing again.

CHAPTER 57

A COMEBACK?

WITH THE extraordinary success of MNF—due in large part to millions of women viewers who previously didn't much care about football—it must have shocked Tex Schramm when Meredith came calling to ask if he could have his old job back.

After one year in the booth, Meredith believed he'd be a better QB than he had been in the past. He likely felt he had some unfinished business.

The answer was no.

Craig Morton was the starter and a rookie from the Navy, Roger Staubach, was waiting offstage.

"I thought I could come back," Meredith said, according to writer Joe Nick Patoski. "I was surprised, but there was very little interest in me coming back.

"Having been away from it for a while, I thought I'd be able to go back and deal with it better."

Schramm, according to Cosell biographer Ribowsky, said, "I think Don had just begun questioning why he'd quit in the first place."

CHAPTER 58

AN EMMY

THROUGHOUT THE 1970s Meredith was one of America's brightest stars. But he was missing several things that would grace his life after he settled in at MNF. One was recognition in the TV industry for his role in revolutionizing football coverage in his first year as a broadcaster. He also met the woman of his dreams.

First the recognition.

There was a game two months into the first MNF season that changed Meredith's fortunes. Arledge let it be known that Meredith was going too far with silly anecdotes. At first, Meredith was hurt, then he handled it correctly. He vowed to be thoroughly prepared for the next game, Cowboys vs. Cardinals.

According to *Monday Night Mayhem*, Arledge told him, "You played with these guys only two years ago. You should really be able to give us great insights—and anecdotes."

He asked Meredith to get inside information from assistant coaches and even Landry, if he could stand to talk to him. So Meredith talked to everyone. He knew the Cowboys strategy for that game plan as if he were still playing.

What happened that night, the *Monday Night Mayhem* authors wrote, "worked because it was utterly unexpected. It was the night that convinced the nation that Monday Night Football was much more about interplay than it was about interference."

Early on, Hayes flubbed a punt.

"Dadgumm-it," Meredith said. "Things like that get the Cowboys into a hole." He realized he was getting emotionally involved and apologized. "Think I'm not biased tonight? Well, I am. But I'll do the very best I can."

Seeing the showmanship of this, Cosell jumped in. He asked the camera operator to get a closeup of Meredith's pain as he watched his old teammates commit one mistake after another.

After a Cowboys punt was run back for a touchdown, Meredith moaned, "There's not that much tackling going on there, boys."

When the Cowboys' offense failed to move the ball, he said, "If we're going to have any fun on this broadcast, the Cowboys are going to have to start playing better ball."

After a Cardinals touchdown: "I'm going to get upset in a minute. In fact, I already am."

Cosell said he wished viewers could see Meredith right then. "He's upset, gritting his teeth. It may make a better picture than the game."

Meredith threw out his game plan: "I had so many funny stories to tell. I can't tell funny stories when something like this is going on."

At halftime with Dallas down 17-0, a chant swelled from the stands: "We want Meredith! We want Meredith!" Fans pointed to the ABC booth.

"No way you're getting me down there," he told the millions watching. "Not on a night like this."

After his Cowboys lost 38-0, he apologized with sincerity about the poor job he did, but Arledge was thrilled. When the ratings came out, the game had beaten a Johnny Carson special shown that night on NBC.

Then the prestigious Emmy Awards were announced. Meredith won an Emmy for Best Commentator in Sports Programming. Cosell was not recognized, and he was miffed. He called Meredith to congratulate him.

Publicly, Cosell's line was "I've got the only Emmy I'll ever need." His wife was named Emmy.

The hurt was still there when Gifford won an Emmy six years later.

Cosell did win his Emmy in 1995, the same year he died.

CHAPTER 59

HIS MARRIAGES

MEREDITH MARRIED his first wife, divorced her, married her again and got divorced a second time. They had one daughter, Mary. He was married to his second wife, Cheryl King, from 1965 to 1971. They had a son, Michael, and a daughter, Heather. He divorced Cheryl in November 1971. He met Susan five months later. They married in July 1972 and were married nearly 40 years.

Susan became his business manager, press agent and chief negotiator. As such, she was a tough cookie who mostly ran his life. He gave precious few interviews. She almost always said no.

For the author of this first full-length Meredith biography, she first invited me to see her, then changed her mind, reverting to old habits.

Meredith delighted in telling how they met. It was April 17, 1971, arguably the best day of his life. He was two years away from football with one season of MNF under his belt. He was walking on Third Avenue in Manhattan when he saw her. He stopped her and they talked, but what he said is unknown.

He liked to joke: "I saw her walking the streets. That's right. A street walker."

He called Gifford and said, "You've got to see this girl."

They all bought kites and spent the day flying them, which isn't easy to do in Manhattan.

Meredith and Susan, now married, along with Gifford became their own team of three. They traveled to MNF cities together, stayed in the same hotel and even got to their favorite cities a day early to see the sights. During games, Susan ordered room service so the boys could eat afterward.

Being in this team of three also allowed them time away from Cosell, who did his own thing in each of the cities. But their closeness made Cosell a little paranoid. He liked to say his two TV partners represented the jockocracy, athletes turned broadcasters, and he had little respect for it. But he knew they had, as he might say, a splendiferous thing going.

Perhaps they did, but seeing her husband's unhappiness, Susan decided to help him make changes in his life. One of them was the possibility of switching networks. He dreamed of becoming an actor.

He was a guest star on the NBC anthology series "Police Story." He wanted to do more, so he and Susan formed Don Meredith Productions.

The authors of *Monday Night Mayhem* called Susan "a strong, shrewd, capable woman." Those qualities would matter as big decisions were about to be made.

CHAPTER 60

THE DEFECTION

WHILE TELLING Arledge everything was fine with his MNF contract negotiations, Meredith and his new agent were talking to NBC. NBC's offer required him to do only 10 NFL games a season, including the playoffs and the Super Bowl, and he could star in made-for-TV movies. He was told he could make pilots for a TV series and possibly even guest host "The Tonight Show" on one of Johnny Carson's nights off.

In contrast, ABC offered him a minor role in a miniseries about Dwight Eisenhower.

When he joined NBC, much to Arledge's dismay, Meredith asked that the nickname Dandy not get used. He considered it a leftover from another era. Dandy Don, he explained, "charms everybody. He's a heck of a guy. But that's not me."

His NBC contract was $400,000 a year for three years. He called football games with Curt Gowdy, a super talent but not one who dreamed of becoming part of a comedy team.

NBC appears to have kept most of its promises. Meredith even got to host "The Tonight Show" in 1975 with Burt Reynolds as a guest.

CHAPTER 61

COMMERCIAL KING

MEREDITH'S HUGE popularity translated into commercial endorsements. That's where the real money was.

For Lipton, as the iced tea spokesman, he bragged about "a dandy tasting tea blend."

He wore a coat in some ads and gave viewers permission to drink the tea all year, not just in the summer.

When that campaign stopped, he replaced it with an 11-year Nabisco contract for $500,000 a year plus a car.

One TV ad showed him dunking an Oreo in ice cream. The campaign's theme song asked, "Who's that kid with the Oreo cookie? It's kind of hard to hide the kid inside when you're clutching an Oreo."

Kmart, Budweiser, Jantzen, Cessna and Winnebago all hired him. Because the money was good, he didn't mind playing the Dandy character.

In a radio ad for an insurance company he started this way: "Texans are known for their bragging. Like the fellow in South Texas who claimed to grow grapefruit so big, it'd only take nine to make a dozen. While in East Texas, they'll tell you their soil is so fertile, if you planted tenpenny nails, they'd grow into crowbars."

After an insurance pitch, he concluded: "Heck, that's worth braggin' about. Because after all, when it comes to braggin' you can always tell a Texan. You just can't tell him much."

Meredith is incredibly popular, so companies line up to hire him as their pitchman. One of his longest relationships is with Lipton Iced Tea. His mandate is to convince Americans to drink iced tea not only in the summer but the rest of the year.

CHAPTER 62

★

THE ACTOR

MEREDITH GOT bit by the acting bug in high school. He never took acting classes (a fact he was later hyper-sensitive about), but his resumé of TV and movies is respectable. He also hosted a longtime football show on Dallas-Fort Worth television.

Joe Nick Patoski wrote, "He was movie-star handsome, now with long sideburns that highlighted his prominent aquiline nose."

He appeared as a guest on TV shows and made several TV movies—"Banjo Hackett: Roamin' Free," "Terror on the 40th floor," "Sky Heist," "Undercover with the

Dave Lieber photo

Probably his most successful acting project is playing the lead in an NBC movie. *Banjo Hackett* was supposed to be a pilot for a possible TV series. It didn't pan out.

KKK," "Mayday at 40,000 Feet" and "Terror Among Us," in which he played a police officer trying to capture a rapist.

He appeared in at least eight episodes of "Police Story" as Detective Bert Jameson. His character was kind and cordial to everyone, victims and criminals alike—not unlike Meredith.

Actor Tony Lo Bianco, who played Detective Jameson's partner, recalled how Meredith "came off as an innocent compared to me, who played a hard-nosed detective." They had a classic good cop-bad cop routine.

Actor Tony Lo Bianco (left) is Meredith's partner in the "Police Story" TV series. Lo Bianco says they had a classic good cop-bad cop routine. Meredith wants to try and be the mean cop, but it doesn't work. He's too nice a guy to pull it off. "It was almost laughable," Lo Bianco recalls.

"One time he said to me, 'Why do you always get to be the tough guy? Why don't I interrogate these criminals and throw them against the wall?' He was really upset.

"So I went to the producers, and I said, 'Listen. Don is really upset. Why don't we give him one of my roles? Let him be the tough guy.'"

They rewrote the script with Meredith as the interrogator.

"I mean, it was almost laughable," Lo Bianco recalled. "It didn't match his personality at all. They changed the script to where I come in and say, 'OK, I'll take over.'

"It became part of the story that he wanted to do this."

Meredith guest starred in "Police Woman," "McCloud," "Supertrain," "Midnight Caller" and "Evening Shade."

He even co-hosted Dinah Shore's show, "Dinah and Friends."

He appeared on stage as the featured player at the 1985 Santa Fe Festival Theatre (the Merediths lived in Santa Fe). Susan was the driving force behind benefit performances of Neil Simon's hit *The Odd Couple*. Her husband portrayed the messy Oscar, and she wanted Robert Redford for the fastidious Felix, but he waved her off.

So she called Frank Gifford.

Meredith and Gifford rehearsed in New York, but the play never played there. "Good Morning America" and "Entertainment Tonight" covered it from New Mexico.

When the production ended, Neil Simon complimented Susan in a note. "Your selection of Frank was brilliant." He credited her with the project's success.

Meredith even appeared in a movie directed and written by his son, Michael, *Three Days of Rain*, which also starred Blythe Danner, Peter Falk and Jason Patric.

His professional acting career lasted from 1973 to 1994, an impressive 21 years. Wonder how good he could have been if he hadn't skipped acting class.

CHAPTER 63

SINGIN' IN THE HUDDLE

MEREDITH WAS a walking karaoke machine, and it didn't take much to get him going. He'd sing at practice, in team meetings, even in football huddles during tense games. It loosened the guys up.

He was heavy on Willie Nelson songs. But his repertoire extended far beyond snippets of Willie's "The Party's Over" on football telecasts.

In 1965, he cut a 45 rpm record—"Travelin' Man" on the A side; and "Them That Ain't Got It Can't Lose" on the B.

I'm a travelin' man
Just a rollin' stone
These wanderin' feet
Have got to roam.

He liked to hang with Jerry Jeff Walker, Roger Miller and Willie Nelson (with whom he sang on stage a few times), and he had half a dozen favorite songs, including "There's a Little Bit of Everything in Texas," "I Didn't Know God Made Honky-Tonk Angels" (his choice in the huddle) and "Honky-Tonk Sweetheart" (favored on the team plane after an away game).

Walt Garrison teased Meredith in his autobiography: "He sold four or five records. I bought two of them and Meredith bought the other three.... If you drank a lot of beer Meredith started to sound pretty good. But it had to be a lot of beer because he was awful."

Decades later, Meredith would play the recording for visitors on his computer and sing along with his younger self.

In 1965, Meredith cut a 45 rpm record — "Travelin' Man" is on the A side, "Them That Ain't Got It Can't Lose" is on the B.

CHAPTER 64

HANK HILL GETS IT

ONE OF THE most poignant tributes to Meredith's career wasn't at a banquet or in a book or a film. It was on a popular cartoon show where Meredith, playing himself, did the voice-over.

A 1999 episode of "King of the Hill" (season 4, episode 6) treated his career with the reverence it deserves, courtesy of Hank Hill.

The cartoon character and the Cowboy were in a contest to throw a football through a tire for big money. Hank asked Meredith to throw for him, and Meredith missed. They ended up talking about the meaning of life.

Meredith: You know, there's something I wanted.

Hank: Don, you have everything....You were a Cowboy during the Landry years.

Meredith: I wanted to go to the Super Bowl. Came close. But it never happened. Never will, and that's all right. I've never looked back.

Hank: It is an honor just to be on the field with you, Dandy Don.

CHAPTER 65

RETURN TO THE MOTHER SHIP

IN 1977 Meredith was back on "Monday Night Football." Cosell reintroduced Meredith to the audience. Meredith said, "I've missed you" and planted a big kiss on Cosell's left cheek.

"I didn't know you cared," Cosell said.

"Ich!" Meredith said, wincing.

Again the request was made to lose the Dandy Don nickname. Cosell stopped for a bit, then resumed using it.

Meredith would explain his return to the mother ship by saying if you're going to perform you might as well do it on the big show on Broadway. He stayed until 1984 for a total of 185 MNF games.

His last game in the broadcast booth was Super Bowl XIX in 1985. It also was ABC's first Super Bowl. His booth partners were Gifford and future Hall of Fame quarterback Joe Theismann, who was still an active player. It was Theismann's first telecast.

Theismann told me how he showed up with notes, clippings, charts and rosters. Meredith arrived empty-handed.

Meredith showed him the fundamentals of color commentary. "You have to speak in sound bites. You can't get off on a long explanation because the next play is coming and you have to give the play-by-play guy—in this case, Frank—a chance to set everything up."

Theismann received a wealth of knowledge that day, and it all soaked in. "Don didn't ramble on, you know? He said what he needed to say and moved out. If I got a little bit long, he would just sorta look at me and sorta grab my hand a little as a nonverbal 'signal to slow down, Trigger, slow down, enjoy the game.'"

Apparently the lessons stuck. Theismann broadcast football games for the next 23 years.

CHAPTER 66

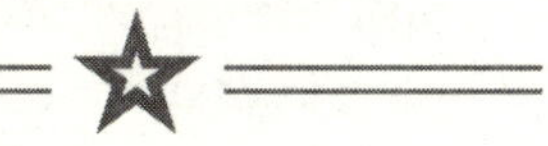

PRIVACY

DID MEREDITH become a recluse?

He mostly vanished from public life.

He and Susan played tennis and golf in Santa Fe. They both learned to paint.

People saw him on the street and cried out "Dandy!" But that was from another lifetime.

His mailbox sported a fake name. He didn't answer the phone but received all messages by fax only.

He's probably the only big-name Cowboy who never wrote a book. It would have been a bestseller.

He refused almost all writers seeking to tell his story.

He didn't respond to old teammates who invited him—by fax—to reunions, which was strange since he was their leader and the life of their party.

Author Golenbock wrote of him going underground: "It's as though he's in the NFL witness protection program."

One theory is he dealt with two of the most difficult human beings who ever walked the planet—Tom Landry and Howard Cosell—and he didn't much feel like reliving it.

Nancy Henson of Greenville, Texas (to whom this book is dedicated because it was her idea), said, "One thing I think is real unusual is how he just disappeared. When he decided to go, it wasn't a retirement tour. It was one and done."

Like most Meredith admirers, "You felt like you knew him even though you never met him. You would have called him Don."

Nancy didn't begrudge his decision. "Leave while you're on top," she said. "Leave them wanting more."

Authentic Meredith autographs are rare because he didn't do autograph shows. He made an exception in 1996 at two Kmart stores in Manhattan. He was buddies with the company chairman.

Asked at the event by a *New York Times* reporter how he spent his time, he answered, "I piddle around."

"I don't miss the limelight, not at all," he said. "I'm just more comfortable out of it.... I have great memories. I feel really lucky."

CHAPTER 67

PAINTING

MEREDITH AND SUSAN found serenity in painting. They painted a lot. When they offered to donate their memorabilia for a hometown exhibit in Meredith's honor, Mount Vernon officials expected sports-related items. Those arrived but so did box after box with paintings by the couple. Nobody knew that he had taken up painting.

All told, the Merediths shipped 150 paintings to the museum. In 2018 the museum put on a show. Some hang in the public area of the museum with the rest kept in storage.

Fruit Bowl is one of many Meredith paintings donated to the
Don Meredith Memorabilia Exhibit at the Old Fire Station Museum.

CHAPTER 68

HOME VISIT

FORTUNATELY, we get a look at Meredith in the final year of his life through the eyes of award-winning *Dallas Morning News* sportswriter Brad Townsend. In 2009 Townsend convinced Meredith—and more importantly, Susan—to let him spend an afternoon with them at their Santa Fe home.

"I lucked out," Townsend said later. "If there's such a thing as a sportswriter's Holy Grail, I experienced it."

He described Meredith as a "supposedly reclusive" fellow who "virtually vanished." Few writers made it inside the house. That only added "mystery and intrigue to an already compelling Texas folk tale."

He showed up at the front door of the house owned by a man who seemed happy to see him.

"Hello, hello!" Meredith welcomed. "Look who's here."

Meredith told Townsend, "Yeah, I'm still here. I did dye my hair, though. Gray."

He didn't travel much because of his need for portable oxygen, he said.

He liked to sit at his computer and sing along with the two country songs he recorded on a 45 rpm record.

He told Townsend how he met Susan on Third Avenue in New York.

Football came up last when Townsend carefully mentioned it. He reminded Meredith that this 2009 interview marked the 50th anniversary of his signing the $150,000 personal services contract that marked the beginning of the Dallas Cowboys.

"Brings back some old memories, boy I'm telling you," Meredith said. "It does, it does. I thank you, thank you."

When people asked Townsend about Meredith's mood, he explained it in two words—happy and peaceful.

CHAPTER 69

IT'S WILLIE

CURT SAMPSON tells this story.

"A phone caller to the house identified himself as Willie and asked to speak to Don," Susan recalled.

"Willie who?" she asked.

"Susan," the man said, "it's Willie."

And for the next 40 minutes, despite the oxygen tube and his shortness of breath, Don Meredith sang duets with Willie Nelson over the phone.

CHAPTER 70

FAREWELL

MEREDITH SUFFERED from emphysema and had a minor stroke in 2004. As his health worsened, he joked that his new nickname was Donny Medicare.

On Dec. 5, 2010, he died from a brain hemorrhage that put him in a coma. He was 72.

In a rare comment to news media, Susan told The Associated Press, "He was the best there was. We lost a good one."

The Texas House of Representatives adopted a resolution hailing Meredith as "a celebrity who transcended sports" and whose "relaxed attitude made him the perfect counterpoint… for the overly articulate Howard Cosell."

He was survived by his brother, Billy Jack; his wife, Susan; his daughters, Mary and Heather; and son, Michael.

He's buried in Mount Vernon, Texas.

CHAPTER 71

AMERICA'S TEAM

BOB RYAN, vice president of NFL Films, was making a Cowboys season film. He wanted a twist on their standard highlights film. "I noticed then, and had noticed earlier, that wherever the Cowboys played, you saw people in the stands with Cowboys jerseys and hats and pennants. Plus, the Cowboys were always the national game on television."

Here's what he came up with: "The Cowboys are the Notre Dame of professional football. No matter where they play, their fans are all across this country. The sum total of their stars are a galaxy. They are the Dallas Cowboys...America's Team."

Their radio network encompassed 10 stations. CBS affiliates in 28 cities carried all their games.

And it all started with Don Meredith.

The coolest NFL cat of them all.

CHAPTER 72

AFTERMATH

THE DALLAS COWBOYS are now the world's most valuable sports franchise worth close to $9 billion.

After Meredith retired, the team played in eight Super Bowls and won five.

After the first victory in 1971, quarterback Roger Staubach said he wished Meredith could be there because he should share in the victory. "This is his team," Staubach said. That's class.

Don Meredith still holds the team record for most passing yards in a single game—460—set in 1963.

Every year Mount Vernon honors young leaders with the Don Meredith Humanitarian Scholarship in honor of Hazel and Jeff Meredith. Don and Susan funded it.

The Don Meredith Exhibit at the Old Fire Station Museum in Mount Vernon is a few blocks from Don Meredith Stadium.

The town christened the museum in 2006 on the occasion of Meredith's 50th class reunion.

Meredith, temporarily not a recluse, cut the opening day ribbon. A thousand people were there.

His longtime friends Ken Greer and Frankie Cooper happily give tours to anyone who asks. On the day I arrived, Greer, a retired banker, was wearing a maroon golf shirt that Meredith gave him.

He recalled that on the museum's opening day, "There was a chair in there for Don, and the crowd just went all the way out the door, across the street and to the backside of what's now The Chop House. I'll never forget that opening." Meredith talked to everyone and signed autographs.

The museum is a beauty. It contains lots of mementos including his Emmy, his childhood basketball and the Bible Tom Landry gave him when Meredith retired. There's a

In December 2006, Meredith prepares to cut the ribbon to
open the museum celebrating his life.

life-sized model of Meredith and his Pro Football Hall of Fame plaque recognizing his lifetime achievement in broadcasting. It's called the Pete Rozelle Radio Television Award. Arledge and Gifford won it, but Cosell never did.

Meredith's jersey on display at the Don Meredith Memorabilia Exhibit at the Old Fire Station Museum. More often than not, on game day it got bloodied.

Dave Lieber photo

Inside the museum is a life-sized display of Meredith.

Howard Cosell died in 1995. He broke ties with most of his friends and died a lonely man.

Tom Landry is a cherished icon having served as Cowboys head coach from 1960 to 1989 when some guy from Arkansas, the new owner who shall remain nameless, went to a golf course in Austin where Landry was playing—and fired him. Southwestern Bell honored Landry by putting his photo on the cover of the 2000-2001 Greater Dallas Residence White Pages. A portion of Interstate 30 is named the Tom Landry Highway, and drawings of Landry adorn the highway walls.

The Cotton Bowl opened in 1930 and still hosts events, including college football. Meredith once said of booing, "I think it's a case of overexposure. I've played more games in the Cotton Bowl than any other guy. I'm a fixture, like the grass."

Meredith never got to play in Texas Stadium with the hole in the roof, which lets God watch his favorite team. But the newly retired Meredith was a big part of the groundbreaking ceremony.

In 1971 Meredith said then, "Here we are in Texas Stadium, which some people call the finest football facility in the world and others call a vulgar display of wealth." Both, he said, were considered attributes in Texas.

Clint Murchison Jr. was finally knocked down and out because his debts caught up to him. To raise cash, he was forced to sell his beloved Cowboys for $60 million. He sold Texas Stadium, which he designed, for $20 million. The buyer was H.R. "Bum" Bright.

But Murchison still went bankrupt. His health failed in his final years, and he couldn't walk or talk. Plus, he lost his favorite business, America's Team.

Tex Schramm resigned before the new owner from Arkansas who shall remain nameless could fire him.

Roone Arledge took over ABC News and turned it into a powerhouse, just as he had done at ABC Sports. He kept control of ABC Sports, too, making him one of the most powerful executives in all of television.

Gil Brandt shared his scouting expertise with other teams and served as a football commentator.

Don Meredith was wearing his high school class ring when he died.

His widow, Susan, now wears it on a necklace.

ABOUT THE AUTHOR

Dave Lieber is a humorist, motivational speaker and columnist who has worked at two major Texas newspapers for 30 years, first the *Fort Worth Star-Telegram*, then *The Dallas Morning News*. As the national award-winning investigative columnist known as "The Watchdog," he advocates for consumers and exposes corruption in business and government to effect positive change.

He is known for his storytelling expertise and for helping companies and individuals craft compelling narratives that engage audiences. He is a certified professional speaker and the author of 10 books and two hit plays. Learn more at DaveLieber.org, DonMeredithBook.com, AmonPlay.com and PerotBook.com.

He also is involved in nonprofit work, cofounding SummerSanta.org, a children's charity in North Texas that for more than 25 years has helped thousands of kids with summer camp scholarships, back-to-school clothing and much more. The accomplishments are especially gratifying as Summer Santa has no paid staff or physical office. For this, Dave was honored to receive the Will Rogers Humanitarian Award from the National Society of Newspaper Columnists. The award goes to a newspaper columnist "whose work best exemplifies the high ideals of the beloved philosopher-humorist who used his public forum for the benefit of his fellow human beings."

ACKNOWLEDGMENTS

For this first full-length biography of Don Meredith, I was fortunate to have two of the most talented editors in the world watching over my shoulder. If there's a better copy editor in American journalism today than John Dycus of Arlington, Texas, I haven't met him or her in my nearly 50 years as a newspaperman.

Same goes for Mede Nix of Grand Prairie, Texas who combined her love of nonfiction storytelling with stories about her favorite football player. She revealed elements of the story that I missed and recommended terrific interview prospects. Her heartfelt introduction gives this book a warm, very human start, and I'm grateful.

I've read a million words about Meredith and the early 1960s Cowboys. The work of several writers stands out.

Curt Sampson wrote a powerful piece in 2010 for *D Magazine* that broke new ground on the Meredith story, especially concerning his infant bout with polio. Curt's report, similar to this book's title, is "Don Meredith: The First Dallas Cowboy." (I added "Dandy" to my title.)

Dallas Morning News sports writer Brad Townsend's accounts in 2009 and 2010 after visiting Don and Susan Meredith in their home is a master class in journalism. The stories are close to perfect.

I am indebted to John Eisenberg, my former colleague at *The Daily Pennsylvanian* student newspaper at the University of Pennsylvania. In the late 1970s, he was sports editor, and I was a columnist. He went on to write two books that captured the early Cowboys in excellent fashion. He was able to interview many of the major figures before they went to Cowboys Heaven.

Of all the players' books I read, one stands out as the most entertaining and informative. Walt Garrison's 1988 memoir, *Once a Cowboy,* contains great storytelling.

Thanks to Russell Maryland, Larry Cole, Joe Theismann, Tony Lo Bianco, Bill Mercer, Garry Hamilton, Ken Greer, Frankie Cooper, Jeff and Amy Briscoe, J.R. Early, Deidra Early, Kelly and Scott Bradley, Nancy George, Nancy Henson, Jon Perry, Randy White, Homer Plankton and Harley Smydlapp.

Thanks to wonderful library archivists Sara Pezzoni of Special Collections, The University of Texas at Arlington Libraries; Elizabeth Johnston of Dallas Public Library's Dallas History and Archives Division; and Joan Gosnell of SMU Archives, DeGolyer Library, Southern Methodist University Libraries.

Thanks to my favorites: TLCBookDesign.com and Tamara Dever (cover) and Monica Thomas (interior).

Thanks to the excellent Franklin County Historical Association and to Dallas Cowboys archivist Jonathan Thorn, who finds answers to tough questions.

Finally, the muse of my life initially was not convinced that this project was worthy, but once she saw the audience reactions as we teased the idea of a book, she came on board and patiently listened to a year's worth of Cowboys stories. My beloved Karen, I love you so.

These people helped me gather all of the scattered material on Dandy Don and bring it to one location. Thank goodness they did. The stories about this man and his life are too precious to lose.

Please. If you're ever near Mount Vernon, visit the wonderful Don Meredith Memorabilia Exhibit at the Old Fire Station Museum.

BIBLIOGRAPHY

BOOKS

Arledge, Roone. *Roone: A Memoir*. HarperCollins. 2003.

Blair, Sam. *Dallas Cowboys, Pro or Con?* Doubleday & Co. 1970.

Carlson, Chuck. *Ice Bowl '67: The Packers, the Cowboys, and the game that changed the NFL*. Sports Publishing. 2017.

Cartwright, Gary. *The Hundred Yard War*. Doubleday & Co. 1968.

Chilson, A.J. *"Dandy" Don Meredith*. A.J. Chilson. 2021.

Cole, Larry. *Living the Dream on America's Team*. Fulton Books. 2021.

Cosell, Howard and Bonventre, Peter. *I Never Played the Game*. Avon Books. 1985.

Cosell, Howard and Herskowitz, Mickey. *Cosell*. Playboy Press. 1973.

Cosell, Howard. *Like It Is*. Playboy Press. 1974.

Dent, Jim. *The Life and Times of [a Cowboys owner who shall remain nameless]*. Adams Media Corp. 1995.

Eisenberg, John. *Ten-Gallon War: The NFL's Cowboys, the AFL's Texans, and the Feud for Dallas's Pro Football Future*. Houghton Mifflin Harcourt. 2012.

Eisenberg, John. *Cotton Bowl Days: Growing Up with Dallas and the Cowboys in the 1960s*. Simon & Schuster. 1997.

Freeman, Denne and Aron, Jaime. *I Remember Tom Landry*. Sports Publishing. 2001.

Garrison, Walt and Tullius, John. *Once a Cowboy*. Random House. 1988.

Gent, Peter, *North Dallas Forty*. William Morrow & Co.1973.

Gifford, Frank. *The Whole Ten Yards*. Ballantine Books. 1994.

Gill, Bob. *Mel Renfro: Forever a Cowboy*. Inkwater Press. 2016.

Golenbock, Peter. *Cowboys Have Always Been My Heroes: The Definitive Oral History of America's Team*. Warner Books. 1997.

Gruver, Ed. *The Ice Bowl*. McBooks Press. 2005.

Gunther, Marc and Carter, Bill. *Monday Night Mayhem: The Inside Story of ABC's Monday Night Football*. Beech Tree Books. 1988.

Harris, Cliff and Waters, Charlie. *Tales from the Dallas Cowboys Sideline*. Sports Publishing. 2006.

Hayes, Bob and Pack, Robert. *Run, Bullet, Run*. Harper & Row. 1990.

Jenkins, Dan. *Semi-Tough*. Thunder's Mouth Press. 1972.

Landry, Tom and Lewis, Gregg. *An Autobiography: Tom Landry*. Zondervan Books and HarperCollins. 1990.

Lilly, Bob and Clark, Kristine Setting. *A Cowboy's Life*. Triumph Books. 2008.

Luksa, Frank. *Cowboys Essential: Everything You Need to Know to Be a Real Fan*. Triumph Books. 2006.

Morton, Craig and Burger, Robert. *The Courage to Believe.* Ballantine Books. 1981.

Murchison, Burk and Granberry, Michael. *Hole in the Roof.* Texas A&M University Press. 2023.

Norman, Pettis Burch. *The Story of Pettis Norman.* SuburbanBuzz.com. 2021.

O'Brien, Michael. *Vince: A Personal Biography of Vince Lombardi.* Morrow. 1987.

Pamplin, Jean and Johnson, Ray Loyd. *Memories of Don Meredith and Hometown Vernon.* Northeast Texas Publishing. 1999.

Patoski, Joe Nick. *The Dallas Cowboys: The Outrageous History of the Biggest, Loudest, Most Hated, Best Loved Football Team in America.* Little, Brown & Co. 2012.

Perkins, Steve. *Next Year's Champions: The Story of The Dallas Cowboys.* World Publishing Co. 1969.

Reeves, Dan and Connor, Dick. *Reeves: A Biography.* Bonus Books. 1988.

Reeves, Jim. *Dallas Cowboys: The Legends of America's Team.* Berkeley Place Books. 2016.

Ribowsky, Mark. *Howard Cosell: The Man, the Myth, and the Transformation of American Sports.* W.W. Norton & Co. 2012.

Ribowsky, Mark. *The Last Cowboy: A Life of Tom Landry.* Liveright Publishing. 2014.

Sheehy, Sandy. *The Big Rich.* St. Martin's Papebacks. 1990.

Sherrod, Blackie. *Scatttershooting.* The Strode Publishers. 1975.

Sherrod, Blackie. *The Blackie Sherrod Collection.* Taylor Publishing. 1998.

St. John, Bob. *TEX! The Man Who Built the Dallas Cowboys*. Prentice-Hall. 1988.

Shropshire, Mike. *The Ice Bowl*. Penguin Group. 1997.

Van Buren, Ernestine Orrick. *Clint Williams Murchison: A Biography*. Eakin Press. 1986.

Walter, Tony. *Ice Bowl: The Game that Will Never Die*. M&B Global Solutions. 2022.

Wolfe, Jane. *The Murchisons: The Rise and Fall of a Texas Dynasty*. St. Martin's Press. 1989.

VIDEOS

Banjo Hackett: Roamin' Free. Columbia Pictures. 1976.

North Dallas Forty. Paramount Pictures. 1979.

Undercover with the KKK. Sony Pictures. 1979.

Don Meredith: The Original Dallas Cowboy. NFL Films.

The Ice Bowl: A Whole New Way of Putting the Game "On Ice." NFL Films.

ARTICLES

Cartwright, Gary. "Don Meredith: More Than Just a Passer." *Sport* magazine. January,1967.

Hoffer, Richard. "Fine and Dandy Don Meredith walked away from two careers at the top of his game, Seldom to be heard from again. (But don't worry about him.)" *Sports Illustrated*. July, 2000.

Kafka, Sherry. "Tuning in Dandy Don." *Texas Monthly*. February 1973.

Kowet, Don. "Backstage at 'Monday Night Football.'" *TV Guide*. November, 1980.

Linderman, Lawrence. "Playboy Interview: Don Meredith." Playboy Press. February. 1978.

Melzer, Richard. "The Dallas Cowboys and racism in America." News-Bulletin.com. 2020.

Sampson, Curt. "Don Meredith: The First Dallas Cowboy." *D Magazine*. October, 2010.

Sherrod, Blackie. "Don Meredith: Can He Prove He's a Winner?" *Sport* magazine. November 1968.

Shrake, Edwin. "A Cowboy Named Dandy Don." *Sports Illustrated*. September, 1968.

Townsend, Brad. "50 Years later, Don Meredith still has a song in his heart." *The Dallas Morning News*. November, 2009.

Townsend, Brad. "The old QB Don Meredith was an unforgettable catch." *The Dallas Morning News*. December, 2010.

In a league by themselves
BIG D's
BIG DOZEN
FORD
DEALERS
present
THE DON MEREDITH SHOW
5:00 P.M. CHANNEL 4, KRLD-TV
Every Saturday afternoon

> *"I won't be remembered as a great passer or as a great signal caller or as a great quarterback. But I hope I'll be remembered as a nice guy."*
> —Don Meredith

Turn out the lights. The party's over.
They say that all good things must end.
Call it a night, the party's over
And tomorrow starts the same old thing again.
—Willie Nelson